T0099853

Spiritual Values in the Workplace

The Soul of Success in the 21st Century

2nd Edition

Cary G. Weldy

BALBOA.
PRESS
A DIVISION OF HAY HOUSE

Balboa Press books may be ordered through booksellers or by contacting:

Balboa Press
A Division of Hay House
1663 Liberty Drive
Bloomington, IN 47403
www.balboapress.com
1-(877) 407-4847

ISBN: 978-1-4525-3906-5 (sc)
ISBN: 978-1-4525-3907-2 (hc)
ISBN: 978-1-4525-3908-9 (e)

Library of Congress Control Number: 2011916283

Because of the dynamic nature of the Internet, any web addresses or links contained in this book may have changed since publication and may no longer be valid. The views expressed in this work are solely those of the author and do not necessarily reflect the views of the publisher, and the publisher hereby disclaims any responsibility for them.

The author of this book does not dispense medical advice or prescribe the use of any technique as a form of treatment for physical, emotional, or medical problems without the advice of a physician, either directly or indirectly. The intent of the author is only to offer information of a general nature to help you in your quest for emotional and spiritual well-being. In the event you use any of the information in this book for yourself, which is your constitutional right, the author and the publisher assume no responsibility for your actions.

Any people depicted in stock imagery provided by Thinkstock are models, and such images are being used for illustrative purposes only.
Certain stock imagery © Thinkstock.

Printed in the United States of America

Balboa Press rev. date: 9/19/2011

CONTENTS

PREFACE

During my tenure in working for Fortune 500 companies, I became disenchanted with the contradiction between what companies said they stood for and what was happening in the workplace. It became apparent that most companies lack heart and soul, and focus on key drivers such as profitability, goals, and competition.

But this isn't how the Universe works, and I felt that there might be some things that we can apply from values that are transcendent. I call these "spiritual values", and you are invited to explore these principles in my first book. In its quiet way of being, the Universe produces more miracles in a minute than a Microsoft, Coca-Cola, or General Electric can produce in 100 years. So perhaps if we get out of our heads and process-oriented thinking for a moment, we can begin to open up our hearts and explore new ways of thinking about our workplaces.

Our natural world and the ways of our ancestors provide real answers for how we can work in a happier environment and produce better results more effectively. Real magic comes from a place of being still . . . doing less . . . and allowing our work that we have all been destined to do to gloriously unfold. And if we shift our attention to "how may I serve", rather than "how much can I achieve or get", then we will fulfill our ultimate destiny: to live our lives in harmony, peace, and exquisite joy.

May your work be inspired in new ways, and may your lives be blessed with love and grace.

From my heart to yours,
Cary

Chapter One

Spiritual Evolution

"We are not human beings having a spiritual experience.
We are spiritual beings having a human experience."

Dr. Wayne Dyer

Corporate America has a reputation for being dog-eat-dog and lacking in spiritual values like generosity, caring, and compassion. During my years in the corporate world, I certainly witnessed a disconnect between the spiritual evolution on our planet and the narrow concerns of business interests. There is nothing inevitable about this state of affairs. Companies can behave with spiritual qualities in mind, and there are many examples of caring and responsibility taking place in the business world. But this trend represents a small portion of what businesses can do to be part of the worldwide evolution of consciousness.

By seeing spirituality in every part of our lives, including our business mindset, we are acknowledging that everything is intimately connected, and we are part of that unity. Mahatma Gandhi said, "I believe in the essential unity of all that lives. Therefore, I believe that if one person gains spiritually, the whole world gains, and that if one person falls, the whole world falls to that extent."

In much of the same way, the whole will function in a manner that reflects how each individual behaves as a spiritual being. The parts and the whole, the individual and the organization, reinforce each other in crafting a more responsible society. This book will focus on developing a spiritual culture in an organization—more specifically, the individual within that organization. By maintaining this personal focus, managers and other leadears can more easily

1

maintain the true purpose and value of the organization. When the individual receives attention and is developed, the entire organization gains.

What are spiritual values? While contemplating spirituality, religion may come to mind. Or others may think of mysticism.

When I refer to spiritual values, they represent a set of values that transcend time and space. In other words, spiritual values apply to any setting, any time period, and any culture. The kingdom of God, as referred to in the Holy Bible, is the realm of spiritual values: those things that are most transcendent. The kingdom of God comes on earth—not in some future apocalypse, but in the here and now of everyday life when people help one another to realize their full potential.

In the 1970s, Abraham Maslow, considered by many to be the father of modern psychology, presented a model that came to be known as "Maslow's hierarchy of needs." The theory is often represented as a pyramid, with basic needs represented by the lower levels and the top point represented by the need for self-actualization. Each level depends on the level below it. That is, a person must have a lower-level need satisfied before moving to the next level. The five-tiered hierarchy of human needs is as follows:

1. Physiological needs (oxygen, food, water, shelter)
2. Safety needs
3. Love, affection, and belongingness needs
4. Esteem needs (self-respect, respect from others)
5. Self-actualization needs (to follow one's calling)

Many people, however, are not aware of his later work, in which he believed that the five-level hierarchy continued higher. He believed that a sixth level was about self-transcendence: a trans-egoic level that emphasized visionary intuition, altruism, and unity consciousness.

The identification of this sixth level resulted from his work in peak experiences and transpersonal psychology, recognizing the human need for ethics, creativity, compassion, and spirituality. Maslow argued that without attention to this dimension in life, our organizations, institutions, and ultimately our society would continue to generate ineffective policies and programs. The discussions throughout this book are in harmony with Maslow's writings in the late '60s and posthumously published work.

Social thinker and University of Pennsylvania Wharton School lecturer Jeremy Rifkin believes that a third industrial revolution is now underway that will lead to a planetary, biosphere consciousness, one characterized by greater empathy for other human beings and smarter solutions to the world's energy needs. In *The Empathic Civilization* (Tarcher, 2009), Rifkin writes that the communications revolution that led to the creation of the Internet was just the opening act of a larger drama that will shift people toward local food and energy production while opening themselves to others on an unprecedented scale. The fragmentation and alienation produced by free-market capitalism will give way to a more sane and livable world, one dominated by the higher end of Maslow's hierarchy of needs.

The impact of an individual ripples outward to a whole organization, a whole society, or the whole world. Think how different literature would be without William Shakespeare or Robert Frost. Think about how Mother Teresa made us all believe that sainthood was still possible; how she cared for the poor, dying, and destitute for decades. Think about how His Holiness the Dalai Lama persevered against all odds, despite the brutality of the Chinese regime.

Our society is evolving toward inner work and inner movement of the individual. Doing things with our mind (at a higher level) is working with a finer level of energy. The finer levels of energy always affect and control the denser levels of energy, both in an individual and in society. So what begins as a thought in one person's mind can change a whole epoch in human history.

In 1897, no one thought that a box could cook food without infrared heat or moving parts. And yet, the microwave exists, and it cooks food at the touch of a button. As I look at the emerging trends, I see more signs that technology will work through the push of the mind, perhaps through biofeedback. Already implants and prostheses can be wired directly to a person's nervous system so that an amputee regains movement through an artificial limb or a deaf person hears again through cochlear implants. Technology and spirituality are coming together to bring us to a level of interconnection that has never been seen before in the history of civilization.

Especially in tough economic times, there is the temptation for companies to scale back programs designed to benefit their employees and contractors. This "race to the bottom" might be advantageous in the short-term, but it stunts the growth of the human capital needed to preserve innovation. Placing value on our most important resources—people—will pay the largest dividends in the long term.

Chapter Two

Modeling Spirituality in Business

"Man's difficulty today is that he is so immersed in the temporal that he has lost sight of the spiritual, has lost sight of God."

Gilbert Shaw
Spiritual Warfare

The movie *Brazil* brilliantly and comically illustrated what corporate America could be like in the twenty-first century: cold, impersonal, hard, efficient, robotic.

In the movie, directives were sent to cold offices via endless miles of mail tubes and computer screens. Executives dressed alike (in suits, of course) marched together in dark, imposing corporate corridors, moving in and out of offices. They conducted business in a clipped fashion, never seeming able to take care of things fast enough.

What was missing in the corporate culture represented in the movie *Brazil*? It was without the human or creative element. It was without spirit. One might even suggest that robots could have played the majority of the characters in the film.

Probably everyone who has watched this film is convinced that the corporate culture had a negative impact on the community around it. People might even suggest that a company set up today in this fashion would probably fail and cause havoc in the world on its way to doom.

What struck me as alarming was that this film exemplifies how a large part of corporate America is run today. I hear so many employees of larger companies complain about how the sense

5

of family has been lost. Most companies do not applaud the individual who stands out from the crowd. In fact, management tends to change the individual and may even ostracize him or her for contrary thinking. This is completely analogous to the suited men who marched together, repeating the same phrases in unison.

Today, many companies have switched to a more casual dress code, and they may allow action figures and family photos in cubicles—but these moves are arguably window dressing. Employees still have little to no control over the way their companies are run than they did before the Internet gestalt shift. So many good ideas simply get squashed or forgotten, because their creators were so stuck in the daily routine of commute, meetings, reports, commute. The daily routine and the organizational structures of typical workplaces kill innovation even without any conscious intent on the part of management.

A more disturbing trend takes place in the physical and emotional deterioration of the lives of employees. The way people approach their work is adversely affecting their health. In fact, more people die at nine o'clock in the morning than any other time of the day. This is astounding! And the human species is the only species that achieves something this remarkable: our very way of doing things slowly kills us.

Subsequently, it is imperative that we change the workplace and ultimately the way people feel about their work. The method of evoking change must involve understanding the larger dynamics taking place in society at large.

Real wages have been declining for average workers since the 1970s, while CEO pay has skyrocketed. As of 2007, the average American worker produced $63,885 in value-added goods and services per year, according to a report from the United Nations' International Labor Organization. Part of this productivity number, the world's highest, stems from working longer hours, but it also results from increased communications ability and organizational streamlining. In other words, Americans have worked smarter and longer than their counterparts in other industrialized nations, but they have not seen a return in the form of higher wages and benefits. In the economic downturn of the last few years, productivity has increased even further as positions are eliminated, and workers have often been asked to make sacrifices in pay and pensions.

The days are long gone when employees could take their first job out of school with a company and plan to retire with that same company. According to the Bureau of Labor Statistics, the average length of time a person works for a given employer was only 4.1 years in 2008, the last year numbers were available. Today's workforce is highly mobile and competitive, rapidly changing and shifting with each new trend. Not surprisingly, many people look for a place of work where they will be more valued rather than just being a disposable resource for those in charge.

With most new businesses failing before ever reaching profitability, perhaps the differentiating factor is the extent to which businesses exemplify spiritual values. After researching many large and small companies, I formulated a model that describes how companies traditionally function versus the spiritual model that I advocate.

Below is the comparison model:

Traditional Company	Model for Spirituality
Driven by sales, profits	Driven by values
What's in it for me?	How may I serve?
Based on fear and ego	Based on love
More tools and stuff	Simplicity
Facts, data	Intuition, feelings
Goals	Process; a way of living
Protective, secretive	Sharing, open
Localized concerns	Universal, boundary-less values
Today	Concern for the future
Here	The environment
Speed	Rhythm and flow
Corporate concerns	Employee concerns
Company culture	Celebrating diversity

Managers, leaders	Creators; everyone leads
Training; teamwork	Inner work for the individual
Plan for the future	Plan less; live in the moment
Processed-focused	Information-focused
Quality products and services	Quality of life
Offices, hallways	Living environment
Meetings, structure	Meditation, creativity sessions

Chapter Three

Focus on Values, and the Profits Will Follow

Seek ye first the kingdom of God, and all of these things shall
be added unto you.

The Book of Saint Matthew
Chapter 6, Verse 33
The Holy Bible

The values and motives of traditional western corporations are
reflected by how they operate. Clearly, the majority of companies
appear to be driven by profits. Business school courses drive this
imperative, which for years have taught that corporations function
only to maximize profit. Unfortunately, for many companies, the
drive to profit strengthens, as those companies face pressure to
deliver performance back to the shareholders. Indeed some legal
decisions, like the one against Ben and Jerry's ice cream, have
forced companies to consider profit above other concerns, such as
environmental stewardship and employee satisfaction.

The cycle can be vicious and unending: last year's performance
is never good enough. Sales for next quarter must be 10% higher
than the previous quarter. This perpetual growth might be
mathematically impossible, but this doesn't stop the insane drive
for "more."

I am amazed at how many companies tie in much of the
compensation of their leaders to the financial performance of
the company. This behavior has a tendency to focus more on the
balance sheet and less on the customers. It drives more internal

meetings, more analysis, and increases fear. It also leads to short-term profitability and the prospect that the CEO will push the "eject" button and float to the ground on a golden parachute while the company crashes and burns.

The madness continues, as divisions will push products earlier on their customers to reach the targets for the quarter or year. But at the expense of their customers and employees, the leaders relinquish their spiritual values for something that could disappear in a brief moment. Just ask anyone who lived through the stock market crash of 1929. That event no longer belongs only to the remote past after the most recent recession, and all of the actions of the Federal Reserve and the government bailouts did not prevent such an event from occurring.

St. Luke's, a communications firm in London, has developed a mission around the work ethics of its people. The company is wholly owned by its employees, and each employee owns a portion of the firm's stock. A five-member council called the Quest governs the firm, and its corporate mission is clear to the world:

> "Profit is like health.
> You need it, but it is not what you live for.
>
> The Treasury monitors the profit we need.
> The Quest monitors the lives we lead."

Saint Luke's defies the expectations of business school curriculum, as its focus on self-governance propels the company to phenomenal growth. This idealistic firm ranks as one of the most desirable employers in London's advertising sector. And it is no wonder. In *everything* that it does, St. Luke's creates ideas as a function of the values of the firm and quality of life of its people. Growth emerges organically from the ethos of the people rather than arising from artificial standards handed down from above.

Many business leaders strive only to amass wealth, regardless of what they might say in a mission statement or annual review. After many years, when they give pause to reflect upon their lives, they often look at their spouses and children and wonder who they are. Realizing that they missed out on experiencing their children growing up and sharing their lives intimately with their spouses, they try, too late, to repair the damage. Spending a lifetime in the office to gain status, power, and wealth ultimately does not satisfy.

More corporate leaders are beginning to recognize the importance of putting their personal lives first, and that the organization comes second. Interestingly, it is becoming apparent that taking care of oneself will result in a more functional and vibrant company. A CEO of an Ohio manufacturing firm valued at over $5 million said, "This year I took only four weekdays off. That's not healthy for the company or for me. My new goal is to take at least a long weekend off every quarter." Another CEO from a company based in Louisiana affirmed, "My 1996 New Year's resolution was that I would take a vacation. In 1997, I'll actually do it." (Source: Inc., Jan. 97, p. 83)

To be certain, delivering value to the shareholders is important. The difference is that it should be the result, not the key driver. "If you build it, they will come," runs the theme in the movie *Field of Dreams*. Follow your dreams, seek out your vision, do what you love, and the rest will follow.

The traditional focus on profits reminds me of bodybuilding. John, who works out regularly each week, lifts weights and runs on the treadmill. He is interested in strengthening his cardiovascular system, building muscle, and increasing muscle tone. Jerry also works out regularly each week, but his primary focus is building muscle bulk. To achieve his objective, Jerry takes anabolic steroids each day, and his body delivers. In just a short time, Jerry's body is rippled with muscle. John, focusing on a more holistic approach, eats with total awareness and ingests foods made as naturally as possible. Over time, John develops a well-toned, muscular physique. He feels energetic and alive.

John and Jerry have achieved the same result: rippled muscles. But their bodies are dissimilar in many ways. John feels energetic and alive. As a result of the steroids, however, Jerry experiences irritability, uncontrollable anger and insomnia. He has a diminished sex drive. His face and back are marked with acne. He has risked his health and possibly his life.

Companies with a bottom-line focus often achieve their results consistently. But their scarred corporate "bodies" have been pushed to produce at the cost of their health. Their energy wanes, reflected by low morale. Some of the functions may even be shutting down. These companies can replace disgruntled employees and may be able to "get away" with short-changing customers, but they are not sustainable in the long term. More and more, investors are beginning to question not only the profitability, but also the ethos of the companies whose stock they buy.

At the same time, Wall Street pays more attention to less tangible elements such as "people factors", the ability of a company to foster loyalty and morale. Conducted by Ernst & Young's Center for Business Innovation, a study involving 275 portfolio managers showed that 35% of investor decisions are driven by non-financial factors. The "ability to attract and retain" talented employees ranked fifth in selecting stocks.

Ernst & Young found that as investors depend more on non-financial information, their forecasts are more accurate. According to Baruch Lev, professor of accounting and finance at New York University's Stern School of Business, only 60% of the average stock's valuation is affected by traditional balance sheet measures, such as earnings. (Wall Street Journal, Feb. or March 1997, front page of Marketplace).

Organizations often relinquish their power to outside forces, such as stock analysts. In one instance, a single analyst had a devastating impact on a company, after he suggested that a division was holding the company's price back. Interestingly, that particular division had achieved record sales and profits that would be deemed incredible by most industry standards. That single statement from the analyst wreaked havoc through the large division, creating fear and uncertainty for its future.

Rather than to focus on potential negative external forces, the central focus of a company should be the customers and taking care of their needs. Too many companies start out by developing a product around the needs of the customer, and then attempt to sell that same product to other potential customers without assessing their needs. Perhaps they don't want Widget A, but need Widget B that is waterproof. This trap of primarily focusing on selling existing products is a result of being driven by cost structure.

Some successes simply can't be transposed or replicated and must be created out of whole cloth.

Customers are increasingly more sensitive to the traditional salesperson who strolls into their offices, eyes glazed with dollar signs, drooling during the handshake, with their open wallets hanging out of the back pocket. "Don't try to sell me something," is the motto of today's skeptical customer. "Simply take care of my needs." Selling happens when customers see that a company meets a need. By developing a strategy entirely around how to make your customers successful, your company will become successful.

You need not always be concerned with making sure that you are getting enough value in exchange for what you are delivering to your customer. That is, spending less time analyzing costs and pricing, and focusing more on delivering your customer's needs will be a winning formula in the long-run.

My parents' company become successful in the plastics industry because they focused on fulfilling their customers' needs. My father delivered products faster than his competitors, and more importantly, faster than his customers expected. He spent little time calculating his costs and evaluating prices and more time balancing the needs of his customers.

Customers do not care much about how "Just-In-Time" your manufacturing processes are, or how many projects you applied Kaizen principles last year. The formula is simple: Take care of their needs, and they will take care of yours.

Let the employees who are closest to the processes figure out how to increase productivity. Reward them for their efforts and achievements. Build this into your culture. Let your employees feel that they are part of taking care of your customers, rather than allowing them to think that they are just attaching some hinges on the widget, or merely inspecting the widget for defects. Be excited about your customer, and the feeling will be contagious.

This universal principle of giving and receiving can be witnessed in every natural process. "Give and it shall be given unto you . . . pressed down." (The Holy Bible, New International Version . . . Luke 6:38)

Chapter Four

How May I Serve?

The true value of a human being can be found in the degree to which he has attained liberation from the self.

Albert Einstein

In Japanese schools, janitors are difficult to find. At the end of each day, the school children clean their respective classrooms, as well as the halls outside the classrooms. This daily habit of self-sufficiency and service becomes a way of life.

And it does not stop there. Each class has its opportunity to serve all of the other students during lunch. The classes rotate on a daily basis, affording each one the honor of serving the rest of the student body.

The idea of service to fellow mankind is a core value in Japan. Restaurants, hotels and department stores are known for their legendary service. Even in the United States, the culture of service prevails in Japanese restaurants. Japanese society naturally instills this important value in early life.

When considering this phenomenon, two questions come to mind. First, why is the value of service to others important? The second question may be more difficult to answer: What can we do to develop this value in a time that rewards self-indulgence? Perhaps the answer lies in looking at what drives behavior that caters to the "self"—the ego.

A Course in Miracles says, "In every moment you have a choice to be a host of God or a hostage of the ego." To understand how to change the focus of an organization, we must first explore the force that drives the force that drives the individual—the ego. However, this discussion of the ego will not deal with the psychological definition, rather the more spiritual approach.

The ego may be defined as the part of the perceptual individual that seeks to identify himself as a separate unit. It is concerned with individuality, judgment, blame, competition, and winning. The ego encourages us to always define ourselves, as it grasps to retain identity, thereby preventing us from witnessing our full potential. For example, while I might see myself as a white male, 172 pounds, author, gardener, and a piano player, such labels separate the self mentally from others.

Transcending the ego requires entering a moment of connection to the higher part of our nature. In those instances of joy or bliss, we experience love, connectedness, peace, joy and creativity.

The game that the ego plays is a game of chase, as the ego pulls the mind toward the game pieces, which are the symbols. The rules of the game are as follows.

The ego struggles to barricade you with symbols. Ego grabs symbols, placing them in front of you one by one, hoping that you will give it attention. As we give the thought attention, the ego runs out to fetch another, and another, until it has created a wall around us. This wall is made up of limiting definitions that are confined to a certain set of parameters:

body	career	garden
money	home	children

The point of this discussion is not to say that anything is wrong with these symbols or their relative importance. Rather, it simply illustrates the mechanics of how we see ourselves through limiting definitions. As we begin to understand the mechanics on the micro level, that is, the individual level, we can apply these principles in business and provide change on the organizational level.

Scientists believe that a person has about 60,000 thoughts each day. The trouble is that over 90% of the thoughts were the thoughts we had yesterday, the day before, and the day before that day. In reality, those thoughts are the individual blocks that form the wall of self-definition.

A new paradigm illustrates who we are: eternal, limitless, unbounded energy. As we transcend this superficial wall, we realize our essential nature. The limiting self-definitions begin to shatter. Those who have meditated have witnessed what Taoists call the "monkey mind", the ego chasing these blocks and tossing them in your path.

Try this experiment. Simple close your eyes. Imagine that you are sitting comfortably in the movie theater of your mind, watching your thoughts played out on the screen. Now let go, allowing your thoughts to be projected onto the screen.

What is your movie about? Nearly everyone reports that their thoughts look something like this:

1) I've got that dental appointment tomorrow at 9 a.m.
2) Wow, my back hurts.
3) Got to pick up the laundry this afternoon.
4) Ooo . . . my nose is itchy.
5) I wonder if I've closed my eyes long enough.
6) This is boring.
7) etc . . . . etc . . .

To escape this endless barrage of "stuff", develop your mind to the point where the eternal, unlimited "you" controls your mind. The Indian sage Ramana Maharshi said, "Reality is simply the loss of the ego. Destroy the ego by seeking its identity. It will automatically vanish, and reality will shine forth by itself."

When the person is healed on deeper levels, the ego becomes less noticeable. The focus turns away from the self and becomes more universal. The individual begins to consider a different question, "How may I serve?"

The Hindus have a word for purpose—dharma. This word dharma describes a sense of devotion to humankind, or duty. We all have a responsibility, or dharma, to some degree of service to our fellow man. Unlike fear-based concepts of divine retribution, dharma is an eternal natural law, one of cause and effect. We cannot opt out of dharma, and embracing it provides a way to increase good outcomes for everyone.

Occasionally, we may be faced with challenging moments during our quest to serve. Opportunities like this exist when a customer turns down an offer or refuses to accept a shipment. When getting a "rejection" from a customer, it is for a reason. Let it go. Meditate on the situation. See if you can identify patterns. In the right moment, the answer to the dilemma will surface.

Chapter Five

Moving From Fear To Love

"The questions asked at the end of his or her life are very simple ones: 'Did I love well? Did I love the people around me, my community, the earth, in a deep way?'"

Jack Kornfield

Dr. Stephen Covey, best-selling author of *The Seven Habits of Highly Effective People*, wrote:

Love in the workplace is the cement that enables all the connections to flow smoothly. Without it, the workplace is a machine without lubricant. Love in the workplace manifests itself in many ways: empathy, respect, courtesies, kindness, keeping promises to other people, never talking behind another's back in a negative way. If you have concerns or criticisms, go directly to the person and share them with an "I" message rather than a "you" message. When you have concerns, you say, "My perception is" or "My feeling is," which is a softer form of giving feedback. It's important to care enough to give feedback to everyone—customers, suppliers, and all your associates inside the company.

The word *love* may be too saccharine for some people in the business context; if so, *caring* will suffice. Sincerity, sacrifice, service, respect, dignity, fairness, and patience are manifestations of love and caring. It doesn't matter what words are used, because the focus is on building good relationships. Relationships in selling, relationships in consulting—they're all about love.

When I began thinking about the subject of love and fear, I smiled to myself, wondering how many people would have red flags go up in response to reading the chapter title. I envisioned how some readers might think of lots of group hugs happening at the office and saying wonderful, loving things all day long. I can assure you that the discussion will be stimulating and interesting. And the applications to your organization will be practical.

I suggest that love can be described as the process of placing one's attention on something or someone without judgment or analysis. To behold or witness without judgment is to accept that object or person without labeling the subject as being right, wrong, good or bad.

We learn to judge and label at a very early age. How many times do you hear a parent tell a child that he or she has been a "bad boy" or "bad girl"? In most cases, that assessment has been linked to an action that may have been carried out, or that the parent does or does not wish to happen. As a result, the child does not want to be "bad", and therefore may not carry out the action that makes him "bad".

By learning that gaining acceptance from our parents is conditional, we develop habits of judgment. Our early role models, our parents in most cases, influence our behavior and thinking as we continue to grow. The concept of conditional acceptance is then transferred from the home to the outside environment, and conditional acceptance becomes the norm for behavior in society, as it has been replicated in most families. John Welwood wrote the following about conditional love:

> This is what we all really want, what our heart wants, what our soul wants—this space to just be. This is also what we wanted from our parents. We wanted them to be present with us. We wanted them to see who we really were. That kind of presence and support is the most valuable thing you can give a child. But instead, what many parents give their children is the message "We love you when you're like this, and we're critical of you when you're like that." That kind of conditional love is a form of control, because it is used as a reward or

punishment. So we grew up learning to do the things we were rewarded for. And that became a prison.

You can continue to live in the prison that you and your parents constructed together, doing things so that you'll get the rewards of "love." But this is like being a rat in a cage, pressing the bar to get food. You keep pressing that bar, trying to get the same empty kind of rewards and reinforcement from other people that you got from your parents, because you didn't get the real thing—genuine recognition and acceptance.

Each person must develop a sense of self-love by practicing the same sort of non-judgment that should be our attitude towards others. We do not need another human being to witness our beauty once we have learned to accept ourselves. The mystery of love for others unlocks once we truly love ourselves.

Fear, the opposite of love, stems from barriers that block the flow of love, usually involving some form of judgment or analysis. If we could spend the majority of our time witnessing, that is loving, without judgment or analysis, we could live in flow without struggle. That place is the point at which "miracles" become common happenings.

Nelson Mandela, in his book entitled *Paper Ships*, said the following:

> "Our deepest fear is not that we are inadequate. Our deepest fear is that we are powerful beyond measure. It is our light, not our darkness, that most frightens us.
>
> We ask ourselves, "Who am I to be brilliant, gorgeous, talented, fabulous?" Actually, who are you not to be? You are a child of God. Your playing small does not serve the world.
>
> There is nothing enlightened about shrinking so that other people won't feel insecure around you. We were born to make manifest the glory of God that is within us. It is not just in some of us: It is in everyone.
>
> And as we let our own light shine, we unconsciously give other people permission to do the same. As we are liberated from our own fear, our presence automatically liberates others."

Nelson Mandela is a great visionary of a spiritually evolving society. And his principles can be beautifully applied to a corporate structure. As individuals in the organization, our spirituality will be manifest to the whole and will liberate others to walk as spiritual beings in the physical universe.

Fear also usually involves a projection into a perceived future time, which necessarily involves an act of imagining or fantasizing. The past and future do not exist . . . they are only ideas, only as real or accurate as the perceptions on which they are founded. Philosophers talk about the "eternal now", in which the present moment is the only reality.

Living in fear often involves our belief about what may happen in the "future", and our judgment relating to what is good or bad about that. A projection into the future typically is based upon our ideas about past experiences, which, in turn, have as much reality as a dream. The German scientist and poet Novalis said, "We are close to waking up when we dream that we are dreaming."

As a valuable exercise, practice watching your thoughts on a daily basis, noticing which ones pertain to the present moment and which ones pertain to the unreachable past or future. Ram Dass said, "Be here now." Practice love in the present moment. The more that love is exercised in each moment, fear has no place to hold.

In the workplace, it is especially important to become aware of attitudes, values, beliefs and behaviors that promote fear, and to strive to eliminate those elements. In his book *Out of the Crisis*, Dr. W. Edwards Deming, the American statistician who revolutionized the way the world thinks about quality, inspired us with the idea to "drive out fear, so that everyone may work effectively for the company."

Fear shuts down people. They freeze, afraid to move or speak. Rather than cultivate a field where people can grow and share their ideas, many organizations reinforce the halls of fear by firing or laying off those who have a new idea of how to do things differently, which may disagree with current styles or methodologies. The curious thing about fear is that it does not promote positive behavior and performance long term. 3M became a great corporation by cultivating an atmosphere of new ideas, supporting those ideas with resources, and rewarding the person who generated the idea.

In a time when bottom line profits are gospel for many companies, the corporate cultures continue to cultivate an atmosphere of mistrust and fear. The ranks become concerned with potential unemployment if the year-end numbers are not met. The lack of trust, a function of fear, may be the #1 problem plaguing our companies. It is the fear that weakens the work force to produce lower results.

Our lives are filled with the "valley" moments in which it may seem impossible to exercise love. John Robbins, Pulitzer Prize-nominated author and son of the founder of the Baskins-Robbins ice cream empire, wrote about the challenge of sharing our love in times that seem most difficult:

> The importance of infusing every action with love became clear to me many years ago, when I was involved in a peace march in the San Francisco Bay Area. The situation became rather intense when the police were called out and tear gas canisters were fired into the crowd. A man walking beside me actually hit an Oakland police officer over the head with the sign he was carrying, a sign that read _PEACE!_ This action has stuck with me as a metaphor for the contradictory desires with which we often struggle.
>
> The key question is, How can we keep our loving centers in the midst of chaos, confusion, and even insanity? How do we work passionately for peace, for example without hating our "enemy"? Perhaps part of the solution to these dilemmas comes from recognizing the central importance of love and from acknowledging the fundamental fact that love begins with ourselves. I may not respect or support someone's actions; I may oppose and in some instances even put my life on the line to stop him or her, yet I will not (if I can help it) allow my opposition to anyone's behavior interfere with my relationship to his or her soul.
>
> I always try to remember that there is pain, suffering, and confusion within each of us. I have no doubt that if I knew other people's entire stories, regardless of their positions on certain aspects of life, I would have compassion and understanding for their predicaments and their choices.

If I knew what their childhoods were like, the turmoil and difficulties they undoubtedly faced, the pressures that impinge upon their goals and actions, the structures of their psyches and how they feel forced to obey certain impulses, I would most certainly feel compassion and love for them, rather than judging them negatively." (Source: Handbook for the Heart, p. 146).

As we see that the basis of spiritual values is our capacity to love, we will open ourselves up to love at higher levels. Throughout our day, whether at home, at work, or at play, opportunities will always present themselves to share our love. These moments may sometimes be challenging, at times where expectations increase.

For example, I have been involved with pricing discussions during negotiations with customers. During these discussions, levels of stress have increased among many of the people present. Barriers of communication go up. Energy does not seem to flow as well.

Through these experiences I learned to practice a technique that I call "sending love." Nearly everyone can sense the anxiety and tension mounting during these types of discussions, due to the expectations and demands placed by each respective business and their interests. When the barriers seem to prevent energy from flowing, I practice imagining love growing inside of my being. As I feel that love expanding, I imagine it flowing to the others in the room, surrounding everyone in the room, circulating freely in the room, and filling the room.

When I practice this during situations that have been traditionally labeled as "tough", something magical begins to happen. The barriers seem to melt away, and the energy begins to flow again. Although the Celestine Prophecy was written as a fictional novel, James Redfield described the process of energy in this manner, suggesting that we would evolve as a society to higher forms by understanding this form of energy. Ultimately, practicing sending and receiving this energy will become a way of life.

The reason why this phenomenon works is simple. While the process may sound goofy, mystical, or crazy, the mechanics of sending love involves the suspension of judgment and analysis.

By removing these elements, we allow the energy to flow. It is like confronting a snake in a corner. As we get closer to the snake, it becomes afraid and forms a coil to protect itself. As we back away from the snake, it no longer feels threatened and begins to relax.

Practice using this technique in situations where conflict may reside. As you work with the method with your mind, you will create a more relaxed environment that will be conducive for better conversation. Freedom will result. As you practice this again and again, you will be amazed how this works.

When I used this concept early on, negotiations with customers relaxed. Both parties seemed happier and walked away from the meetings more content.

This concept is about doing more with less. It is the way we are evolving, where thought is directly connected to the results. We can truly accomplish more by exercising our love in every moment of our lives. The poet Rainer Maria Rilke expressed it well:

> "For one human being to love another human being: that is perhaps the most difficult task that has been entrusted to us, the ultimate task, the final test and proof, the work for which all other work is merely preparation."

Chapter Six

Simplicity

Our life is frittered away by detail . . . simplify, simplify.

Henry David Thoreau

Having worked for a number of small and large companies, including several Fortune 500 companies, it has become evidently clear that simplicity is key. We need fewer "tool kits". Many corporations, for example, have numerous training programs, including Kaizen techniques, productivity sessions, customer-needs mapping, etc. for employees.

Such programs have their merits, but they leave employees confused and overloaded with information. The question becomes, "Which method or strategy should be used with the customer?" Ultimately, these efficiency methods stifle creativity, and the employees lose focus on the customer. The number of internal meetings increase, and the number of customer meetings decreases. Consequently, employees spend large amounts of time training and retraining for these programs, and less time with customers.

The key is balance. Use only a few tools, the fewer the better. Use only the essential tools. Avoid analyzing which tool is appropriate for the session. In the long run, it is probably better to avoid tools and just get into the flow of the moment, allowing your creative energy to solve the issues.

Philosopher William Barrett warned in 1978 of "the illusion of technique" in his book of the same name, saying that the tools that we use to perceive reality can get in the way of perceiving reality itself. People become captive to their own techniques, devotees of the next intellectual trend, and this is nowhere more true than in management literature.

Nature is simple. It becomes increasingly complex only as we begin to analyze "how things work". But it is not critical that we understand the hows and whys. Being true to reality sometimes involves subtracting layers of complication and not adding more techniques, more jargon, more processes.

One company practiced simplicity through a process called "Workout". Everyone in the company was encouraged to examine how work was done. Each person was given a red rubber stamp to imprint unnecessary reports and circulated memos with the message "This is unnecessary. Please do not distribute". The employees were able to return the material to the sender without fearing consequence.

"Workout" also involved creativity sessions where employees were rewarded for simplifying, and thereby eliminated cost. Moreover, the management assured the organization that no jobs would be lost in the process. As a result of Workout, the company saved millions in overhead, as well as direct labor and materials. The employees felt empowered, as they were part of the process.

More can be accomplished by doing less. Nature is not about struggle. We can work smarter by allowing the universe to work for us . . . it is far better at organizing the details. Simply visualize the desired outcome, then relinquish your attachment to the outcome. Attachment is about the fear of loss, which deals with the struggle for the ego to retain its identity.

Growth can be achieved effortlessly. A business can grow naturally. This does not imply that work is not performed, rather struggle is absent. Growth should be practically effortless. Witness the amazing power of nature. It does not struggle to produce the most beautiful flowers. Nor does it struggle to create a baby. A plant can split a rock in half.

Chapter Seven

The Power of Intuition

Truth is not far away. It is nearer than near. There is no need
to attain it, since not one of your steps leads away from it.

Dogen Kigen
Zen master

Scientific theory has historically been the basis for moving
technology forward. Once proven, a theory becomes fact.

The problem with this traditional model is that it is grounded
upon perception through the five senses. "Prove it to me" and "I'll
believe it when I see it" are typical expressions of how much we rely
on our senses to guide us.

When we rely solely on data, pie charts, line graphs, bar charts,
and so forth, we deal only with the past and not the present. How
did we do last year? The previous year? Last quarter? How was our
performance last month? What was our inventory last week?

Data dies the second it hits the spreadsheet: yesterday's news
becomes the basis for tomorrow's forecast. "The trend shows
that sales are expected to climb 10% over the next eight months."
While some analysis is important, too much will inhibit growth.
Remember the adage, "analysis brings paralysis."

Trends and forecasts based on yesterday's results limit how the
emerging future can be perceived. As we mark the boundaries of the
territory, people seem to live in the confines of that thinking. The set
parameters become the ceiling for performance. Our imaginations
become victims of the constraints of our own analyses. Ultimately,
we become in danger of under-performing, because real growth
happens in the here and now.

To manage the movement of circus elephants, trainers will often tie a chain around the leg of an elephant. If the elephant tries to wander away from the area, the elephant will feel the pull of the chain, as the other end of the chain is secured to a large tree, for example. After a while, the elephant learns the roaming distance, as the chain prevent the large animal from going beyond the length of the chain.

Curiously, if a flimsy rope is substituted for the chain, the elephant's behavior does not change. It may stroll up to the point of the length of the rope. And while the strong elephant could easily break the rope and run away, the elephant does not.

A fish in a tank will react in much this same way. If a panel of glass is placed in the center of the tank, thereby creating half the space for the fish to swim, the fish becomes accustomed to its limitation. After a period of time, the glass may be removed, but the fish will not go beyond that point where the glass once was.

An interesting example of how measuring data and facts can be counterproductive was cited by John Naisbitt and Patricia Aburdene in their groundbreaking book Megatrends 2000. Naisbitt and Aburdene pointed out that the trade deficit in the United States is no longer a deficit. Trade is measured by the number of tangible products that are exported out of this country. The issue is that intangible items such as financial, consulting and computer services are not included in the government-published figures. Consequently, public alarm is raised when the trade deficit numbers reflect how well or how poorly America is doing with respect to other countries. Naisbitt and Aburdene argue that if intangibles were included in these figures, the trade "deficit" would disappear.

I might suggest that it is inconsequential to attempt measuring the balance of trade. With the dizzying speed of change relative to the information industry, it is virtually impossible to measure who is selling what information to whom, at what time, and determine how much that information is worth. Clearly, this anomaly demonstrates how our more universal world is dissolving the need for measurement and analysis. Businesses that wait for analysis will always be behind the curve, while those who put innovation first will always be ahead of it.

As we continue to evolve, we are moving toward multi-sensory perception, a step beyond relying only on the five senses. It is trusting your higher self, that natural and innate force within each of us that connects to all that exists. Call it intuition, your gut instinct, or whatever you choose to label it. It is arising within you to guide you beyond what you see, hear, touch, taste and smell.

When you rely on that intuition as a guiding force, it will be apparent that your five senses occasionally fool you, but you will always be able to trust your "higher self", or that intuitive force within you.

Being guided by your feelings is quite different than guided by emotion. Emotions are reactions to something that is external to you. They are pulses of energy initiated by fear or excitement. Friends who have not seen each other for years feel overwhelming emotions of excitement. Emotions are relatively short-lived, as they come and go. Feelings, on the other hand, arise from the inner quiet and calm. Our true instincts, as we become connected with them, are always correct. The power of trusting our feelings, or instincts, is that we will always be guided in the appropriate direction.

For many, it will feel uncomfortable at first as the process unfolds of trusting intuition and relying less on the five senses. An "ungrounded" feeling bubbles up when listening for that intuition.

The process that will need to occur will be getting grounded to the force that connects us all. It is that field in which all truth exists, the place beneath conscious thought, beneath language.

The paradigm will shift from being grounded in "fact" to being grounded in less tangible forms. Keep in mind that what masquerades as fact is no more grounding than feeling or intuition. Quantum physicists have learned that material form is not as concrete, stable or permanent as we have believed for centuries. For example, if you examine a rock and begin to look at what makes up that rock, it will lead you to smaller units of matter. Molecules will lead to elements, and elements to atoms.

Consider the atom. It is 99.9999% empty space. Not air. *Empty space.* The electrons and neutrons on the atoms are made up of smaller energy particles, and from there, it becomes very nebulous. The particles or waves are fluctuations in time and space. In short, the interesting thing about matter is that it changes form depending on how it is being observed.

The Internet illustrates how quickly our world is changing. The knowledge contained in the world doubles in less than a year. Technology evolves in lightning speed. Within months, computer models become obsolete. News that is a day old is old news.

We can no longer afford to ground ourselves completely on what we have traditionally considered to be "reality." It shifts too rapidly. On the other hand, we are expanding our abilities to trust this deeper part of ourselves that transcends facts, data, and analysis. The writer Henry Miller wrote:

> I obey only my own instincts and intuition. I know nothing in advance. Often I put down things which I do not understand myself, secure in the knowledge that later they will become clear and meaningful to me. I have faith in the man who is writing, who is myself, the writer.
>
> (Source: Miller, Henry, "Reflections on Writing," *Wisdom of the Heart*, Norfolk, Conn., New Directions, 1941 (repr. In Ghiselin [ed.], *The Creative Process*, Berkeley, University of California Press, 1954).

For a moment, think about someone who professes his or her love for someone else. Ask that person how does she know that she is in love. She will simply reply, "I just know it. I can't explain it. I just am."

In much of the same way, this type of "knowingness" will redefine how we ground ourselves in life. Our decisions will be based more on our intuitions. You and your organization will be making more and more choices based on this new paradigm of spiritual grounding. Deepak Chopra has said to "go with your gut, for your gut cells have not evolved to the point of doubting."

When I first began to trust my instincts, the results were very surprising to me and my co-workers. One particular customer, Rachel, was working on several key projects at her company. Usually Rachel was very busy with internal and external meetings.

Consequently, she was difficult to reach by phone, as she was rarely at her desk.

Many of our team members would attempt to call Rachel several times a day for several weeks. The frustration began to build in our group, as progress on our development program lagged, and program timing slipped.

As I began to tune in to my intuition and learned to experience the subtle feelings as they bubbled up, I started to get flashes of Rachel in my mind from time and time. Whenever she came to mind "out of the blue," I felt like it was time for me to call her. The unusual would happen . . . Rachel would answer the phone at his desk . . . *every time.* Our team was absolutely dumbfounded that I could reach her.

It demonstrated the extraordinary power of trusting your higher self, the part of you that transcends space and is connected to all that is. Trusting in this Self requires a leap of faith, but it can have the most amazing results once this true nature becomes a guide.

Chapter Eight

The Transition from Goals to Process

If the place I want to arrive at could only be reached by a ladder, I would give up trying to arrive at it. For the place I really have to reach is where I must already be.
What is reachable by a ladder doesn't interest me.

Ludwig Wittgenstein
Austrian philosopher

Goals. Nearly every motivation speaker preaches goals as the way to attain success. Having no goals, they say, is like trying to reach a destination without a map.

Let's examine the process of formulating goals, and the aspects of achievement. A goal must have the following elements:

1) Quantifiable and measurable
2) Time-based
3) Achievable

The life lesson that has emerged for me is that the pursuit of goals can be one of limitation and disappointment. I have witnessed, for example, people who have wanted to lose weight. Someone may state a goal to lose 40 pounds by March 1. Certainly, this statement has all of the elements of a goal. It has a measurable target. It is has an element of time. And it may even be achievable. It focuses a little too much on results instead of process, though, which is a sure road to disappointment.

Forming goals suggests that happiness will result by achieving the goals. Or other people will be happier if the goals are reached..

Or other people will be happier the goals are reached. The focus on the outcome gives birth to disappointment. Instead, getting into the *process* has resulted in my personal growth. I have felt enlivened by getting into the flow, and by letting go of the result. Process has a certain momentum of its own that leads to still more creative activity.

Setting a certain number of limits holds back the greatness that can be achieved. The same holds true for determining what is achievable. How do you know what you can achieve? Someone was once asked, "Can you play the violin?" He replied, "I don't know. I never tried." Merely dreaming up plans does not lead to success: actual work, however halting, does.

And what is time? Why all of the pressure to achieve that something by a certain time?

A top goal for many companies is to be the #1 company in their industry. Many leaders equate being the best with being at the top and having the numbers to prove it. Competing to be #1, however, will become increasing difficult, if not impossible. The first problem is measuring what "number one" means. As technology continues to increase market segmentation, measuring will become harder. The business landscape changes all the time, and what leads to the number one slot today spells disaster tomorrow. General Motors, for example, got so invested in the SUV trend in the 1990's that they lost the emphasis on fuel efficiency that would be needed going forward. Focusing success too narrowly can lead to this sort of reversal.

The quality guru Dr. W. Edwards Deming, in his "14 Points for Management" that serve as the foundation in all aspects of doing business, discussed the importance of eliminating management, stating that it was critical that companies eliminate work quotas and standards on the factory floor. Instead, Dr. Deming suggested organizations substitute <u>leadership</u> as the driver for change. He also believed that the responsibility of supervisors must be changed from sheer numbers to quality, a paradigm shift from goals to less quantifiable and tangible elements. Without the strait-jacket of quantified results, managers and employees can make creative decisions that nimbly adapt to changing conditions.

Consultants and trainers hail the popular study of the Class of 1953 at Yale University as a benchmark that proves the effectiveness and power of setting goals. Researchers purportedly surveyed the graduating class of 1953 to identify the number of seniors who had specific, written goals for their years to come. The results of the study indicated that 3% of the class had goals. After twenty years, the researchers discovered that the 3% with goals had amassed more wealth than the rest of the 97% combined!

The fascinating element of this story is that the study *never occurred*. As a researcher began to delve into those who repeat this "study" as gospel, he began to discover that no evidence existed to back it up. This researcher also talked with graduating members of the Class of 1953, and discovered that they never participated in any study on personal goals. Interestingly, current CEOs of companies predicted future careers, many of which were quite different than their previous ambitions. Yale University finally researched the archives for evidence of the study and came up empty-handed.

While this "study" is completely fictitious, the possibility still exists that goals yield results. I have not seen any research to prove this. On the other hand, the "progress" in my life has been a result of the opposite of the goal-setting process, that is, *not* having goals.

My significant career advances were made entirely by not planning and not pursuing the "next move." Rather, those achievements occurred unexpectedly through amazing circumstances. Miracles can occur in life every day, if we learn to let go and let them simply happen. Focusing on taking the opportunities as they come will be more important in the long run than trying to make life conform to our plans.

Timeless words remind us that "the journey is more important than the destination." Likewise, the process is more meaningful and rewarding than the goal. The destinations, or the goals, will pop up along the journey.

By continually focusing on the result, through setting goals, one projects into the future. The idea is to live for today, and get into the process, living out each moment as it comes to you. The ironic thing is that results will intermittently occur, popping up from time to time. The outcomes will be more spectacular and more timely than what you can even imagine. Just when you feel defeated, you will have enough of a victory to keep your enthusiasm going.

It takes one thing . . . having the thought of what you intend to happen as the result, and letting go to let the universe bring it to you. That is not to say that no effort will be involved in the process. You need to work to produce the result, but you have surrendered control over the outcome.

The difference is that you will become more attuned to knowing what you need to do. Inspiration will come to you more frequently, and the resources will be made available to you. The universe we live in is one that flows. Getting into the process is about getting into the flow. The results will happen in their time.

Allowing things to happen means not abandoning proactivity. The Taoist tradition teaches that the yin and the yang, the masculine and feminine, inhere within one another. So effort must be balanced with surrender, creativity with self-discipline, emotion with rationality. The rare person who masters this secret can work indefinitely without tiring, because she has learned to cooperate with the universe rather than working against it.

Western culture has promoted the belief that to achieve, we must make things happen. The latest findings, however, indicate the importance of balancing these two opposites. For most "achievers", this translates into cultivating the feminine nature and allowing things to flow. For those who undermine themselves by under-working, a little bit of passionate action leads to overcoming past inertia.

Martial arts demonstrates the dynamics of how these opposites interplay to produce results. An observer might at first believe that the masculine nature is producing results. A right punch. A kick from the left foot. An elbow strike to the head. Upon closer examination, it will become obvious that the martial artist is getting into the quiet, intuitive flow. The masculine nature, perhaps in the form of a punch, will arise as part of that flow. While practicing, the delicate balance becomes the objective. And it is the search for this balance that becomes our spiritual journey. Sometimes bending can achieve more than pressing forward: sometimes softness works better than hardness.

It is often surprising at how these "spiritual" aspects play an important role in every part of our lives. For example, I began weight training with Pat Smith, a personal trainer in the Detroit area, who shared many of the spiritual principles in her life. A series of synchronistic events pulled us together, telling me that training with Pat was the "right" thing to do. Most people who are engaged in weight training are probably wanting to develop strength and muscle tone. But training with Pat was surprisingly holistic, in that opportunities arose to move beyond fears and release emotional energy that had been blocking progress in my life. I simply got into the flow of the process and listened.

Spend more time allowing inspiration to permeate your being. Simply let go, and listen to the messages from the universe. Learn to trust your instincts, your intuition, your higher self. Begin to work in a deeper mode, that part of you that already knows exactly what to do.

Chapter Nine

Opening Up to Sharing

The wise man does not lay up treasure.
The more he gives to others, the more he has for his own.

Lao-Tze
The Simple Way

The traditional company in many ways reflects the egocentric persona, striving to maintain its identity and protect its territory. Preservation of self is accompanied by a secretive unwillingness to share. To share information, knowledge, material possessions, status, power and prestige.

Children learn this behavior at an early age, probably at about two or three years of age. They begin to say, "That's mine," and throw a holy tantrum if the parent encourages the child to share with his playmates.

While that sort of behavior apparently vanishes as the child matures, adults still act in much of the same way. Toys become material possessions or friendships. Status, power and prestige become the buried treasures that are sought after, as the ego travels on its expedition to bring back the gold for self.

Companies, in their struggle to remain fiercely competitive, personify the same characteristics. Information becomes the prized possession in the quest to be #1. Managers typically share information internally on a need-to-know basis at best. Sharing knowledge with anyone outside the company is often taboo. That would lead to competitive suicide. Or would it?

Several companies have learned that by sharing information with customers, position in the marketplace is strengthened.

Some companies are providing customers with on-line access to instantaneous quality data on their manufacturing processes. Furthermore, those companies share office space with customers to discuss openly how to improve quality and service.

The business culture across the globe has begun to shift. Just as the Berlin walls that once divided countries have tumbled, the walls dividing companies as separate entities are crumbling. Companies are forming strategic partnerships, moving away from separate primes or suppliers, to becoming a networked set of organizations capable of responding quickly. Businesses are learning the tremendous power of leverage by sharing resources.

This phenomenon has also begun to transform the religious world. The proliferation of religious sects and organizations continue to diminish, as leaders are coming together to discuss areas of similarity. This focus is reflected in how churches are becoming decidedly more similar, leaving behind some of the rules and formalities that have served as barriers for centuries.

The incredible shift of sharing information, once considered to be breaking competitive law, will produce accelerated growth in new knowledge. We are headed in the direction that was pointed out in the film Star Trek First Contact. While escaping the terror of the Borg, the woman from the 21st century asked Captain Jean-Luc Picard about his motivation in space travel. Captain Picard responded that in the 24th century the prime motivation is not profit. Rather, society is driven by the need to evolve as beings.

While one might first think sharing "competitive" data might lead to vulnerability, the opposite happens: the process of sharing creates an environment of trust as fear is abolished. Trust leads to open dialogue, and creativity invariably flows like water. The result is positive, and solutions bubble up to delight the customer and supplier alike.

In the future, managers will focus on creating shared resources with their organizations, recognizing the power that is associated with having those resources available to many. Leaders will also be charged with identifying potential barriers that prevent the sharing and utilization of resources.

This new paradigm has the ability to move beyond mere "synergy," where corporations come together for mutual benefit, to a more open-ended form of cooperation in which the benefits are not calculated beforehand. As "me" and "mine" diminish, the need for protective, defensive action will also diminish, making room for more creative and spontaneous action.

This aspect of sharing will also dramatically impact the necessity for union representation. As companies become more global, their interests will expand beyond their traditional priorities to encompass the needs of their employees, and how their actions affect the world. Corporate giants are becoming fewer and smaller. Small and medium-sized businesses are booming. Establishing unions will become increasingly unnecessary as the resulting higher competition will drive smaller companies to become more sensitive to the needs of their employees. It will also be difficult to establish unions at smaller companies, as more resources are required.

Chapter Ten

The Emerging Open and Boundary-less World

As a mother at the risk of her life watches over her only child,
so let everyone cultivate a boundlessly compassionate mind
toward all beings.

The Buddha

Companies today discuss their role in the world of business.
Marketing strategies revolve around how they will do business
around the globe. Corporations recognize the importance of
setting up manufacturing facilities to position themselves in a
worldwide market. The term "world-class quality" is being spoken
by companies in a race to climb to the top of the competitive
heap.

Business leaders are now shifting their focus to values as a basis
for going beyond the physical aspects of global conquest. Many
are recognizing the need to act for the greater good of all, placing
this at the core of key decision-making processes. Companies are
aligning their principles to work with the laws of nature.

In the movie *Star Trek 2*, Spock sacrifices his life to save the ship
Enterprise. While dying, Spock tells Captain Kirk, "The needs of
the many outweigh the needs of the few, or the one."

This selfless attitude is becoming more present among
organizations worldwide. We are recognizing that there is something
greater than the how profitable our company will be this year, or
how large the Gross National Product will grow this quarter. The
common threads that run through us all are those spiritual fibers

that weave the meaning of our lives. These elements of our eternal nature are becoming the priorities in our work and play.

Consider the possibilities of focusing more on these values in our homes, in our schools, in our stores, and in our companies. What would happen if the media suddenly spent as much time discussing world peace or feeding the children as they spent covering the recent royal wedding or Donald Trump's presidential bid?

Lifetime Television is devoted to programming for women. ESPN is about sports programming. MTV and VH1 broadcast music videos to the world. I am looking forward to the debut of a worldwide television network dedicated to personal growth and spiritual evolution. Perhaps Oprah has something like this in mind with her new network: it remains to be seen what impact this will have.

Companies are expressing values of a more global nature. With over 1400 shops in 46 countries, founder Anita Roddick of The Body Shop, that produces and sells skin and hair care products, devotes much of her focus to universal values. She says the following in the company's web page:

> "I'm in the skin and hair care business—an industry that at times seems hell bent on promoting unattainable ideals. I've often wondered when looking at the industry why it portrays female flesh as gross, never men's? Why don't they celebrate the change of flesh? The aging of flesh? Why is perfection and youth always what is needed? Why do they think of wrinkles as some kind of 'disease'?
>
> How come the 'beauty' industry can spend time fashioning phony medical conditions such as cellulite, and aging—natural processes that occur in all women—and yet fail to make the link between smoking and cancer? And why do the beauty magazines devote thousands of column inches to cellulite rather than exposing the tobacco industry?
>
> Well, enough is enough. We're going to do something awareness-raising on behalf of self-esteem and self-authority. We will be challenging the cultural conceptions of femininity as portrayed in the 'beauty' industry. We will be working hard to promote self-esteem, cultural and physical diversity. We will encourage the celebration of unique qualities that make each

of us what we are. Self-esteem is truly the route to revolution. We are not in the habit of making the connection between self-esteem and democracy, dignity, political activism and freedom of self-expression, but in the future we will be."

These are striking words from a corporate leader whose company has successfully sold skin and hair care products without "resorting to sex, glamour and hype." The Body Shop message is "Celebrate yourself and love your body." They truly are transcending the elitist and agist thinking that has permeated our society for centuries by proclaiming traits such as character, vitality and high self-esteem make the person beautiful.

This solid company reaches beyond its marketing efforts to make the world a better place. It has displayed strong leadership in the call to end the testing of products and ingredients on animals. The Body Shop has also been heavily involved in addressing domestic violence issues, and escalated its campaign of compassion to secure justice for the Ogoni people of Nigeria, following the execution of their leader Ken Saro-Wiwa. In June of 1996, The Body Shop joined an ad hoc working group, including Tesco, Lloyds Chemists and IKEA, to address increasing public concern over PVC and the impact of dioxins and phthalates on human health and the environment. IKEA and The Body Shop have joined numbers of companies in removing PVC in primary and secondary packaging from retail items.

Other companies are basing their philosophies on spiritual values. Ben & Jerry's Homemade, Inc., the maker of premium ice cream and frozen yogurt, is dedicated to the creation and demonstration of "linked prosperity." Its Statement of Mission consists of three interrelated parts: product, economic and social. Ben & Jerry's has identified with the new corporate paradigm that recognizes the interdependence of these elements, and the corporation follows its mission with dedication:

1. Product. To make, distribute and sell the finest quality all-natural ice cream and related products in a wide variety of innovative flavors made from Vermont dairy products.
2. Economic. To operate the Company on a sound financial basis of profitable growth, increasing value for our

shareholders, and creating career opportunities and financial rewards for our employees.

3. Social. To operate the Company in a way that actively recognizes the central role that business plays in the structure of society by initiating innovative ways to improve the quality of life of a broad community—local, national, and international.

Each year, Ben & Jerry's gives away 7.5 percent of its pre-tax earnings to support projects which model social change—projects which "exhibit creative problem-solving and hopefulness." One of the three avenues for giving, the Ben & Jerry's Foundation, is managed by a nine-member board and reviews proposals relating to children and families, disadvantaged groups, and the environment.

This forward-thinking company supports causes such as Vermont Children's Forum, a nonprofit, nonpartisan research and advocacy organization that focuses on the full spectrum of child and family issues. Ben & Jerry's also encourages the participation in Project Vote Smart, the one-stop shopping center for political information. Project Vote Smart is also a nonprofit and nonpartisan organization. Ben & Jerry's rallies consumers to tell Washington to invest more in services for children and to cut back on wasteful defense spending through Business Leader for New Priorities.

The ice cream company has taken a strong stand against the use of rBGH (Recombinant Bovine Growth Hormone), a genetically engineered copy of a naturally occurring hormone produced by cows. The drug is manufactured by Monsanto Company and is sold to dairy farmers under the name POSILAC. When rBGH is injected into dairy cows, milk production increases by as much as 15%.

Unfortunately, the drug rBGH causes serious health problems in cows, including udder infections, a greater need for antibiotics, reduced pregnancy rates, cystic ovaries and uterine disorders, digestive disorders and lacerations, and enlargements and calluses of the knee. The drug also decreases the levels of protein in the milk and causes the milk to sour earlier.

This artificial drug is not necessary. U.S. dairy farmers already produce more milk than the public consumes. The primary purpose is to increase profitability for larger dairy farms, at the risk of smaller family dairy farms, the cows, and human health. Ben & Jerry's not only believes in using milk and cream from cows that have not been treated with rBGH, the company challenges laws that prohibit food manufactures from using labels that explain the use of milk and cream from rBGH-free cows.

This example clearly illustrates the need for public outcry. We must refuse to manufacture products that are harmful to our planet. We must boycott products that produce pain and suffering at the gain of an extra dollar. We must voice these critical issues to our politicians that represent us at the local, state and federal levels. We must demand reform by the federal Food and Drug Administration to require truth-in-labeling of food products that contain potentially harmful ingredients, or ingredients produced from processes that are unfriendly to the environment.

Chapter Eleven

Embracing Our Planet Earth

Every part of this earth is sacred to my people. Every shining pine needle, every sandy shore, every mist in the dark woods, every clearing and humming insect is holy in the memory and experience of my people.

Chief Seathl
Letter to the President of the United States
1885

Taking care of our planet is a spiritual act. The environment is an extension of our bodies. It is part of who we are. We must nurture our environment, as Mother Earth requires loving care.

Between 1990 and 2004, the amount of trash recycled in the United States almost doubled as more companies, universities, and homes began recycling programs. Many municipalities began curbside pickup, and less wasteful packaging became a selling point for products. The story of recycling over the past two decades signals that people can change their ways if enough effort goes into viable alternatives. There are still areas where we can build on this success.

Americans throw away over 2.5 billion pounds of batteries each year. These batteries contain toxic heavy metals, including mercury, cadmium, zinc, nickel, lead and lithium. Mercury and cadmium then leach into our groundwater from the landfills, and pollute the air with toxins when the batteries are incinerated. Mercury toxicity has been linked to cancer, as well as other health problems. Using rechargeable batteries, which don't contain the same chemicals, last longer and pay for themselves.

Companies need to be more prudent in targeting mailings at the homes of consumers. Americans toss out over *2 million tons* every year, an equivalent of 1-2 trees per household each year in junk mail. Much of it is never opened. Consumers can write companies asking them to stop, and ask large direct-mail companies, such as the Direct Marketing Association (Mail Preference Service, 6 East 43rd Street, New York, NY 10017, www.optoutprescreen.com), to remove their names from mailing lists.

Design for Environment (DFE) is fast becoming a part of the product and process design. Addressing environmental concerns in the initial phase reduces the overall cost associated with the waste stream. DFR, or design for recycle, allows products to be broken down at the end of their useful life and recycling the individual products for use in other processes. Designing for disassembly (DFD) is an effective tool that assists in these other processes.

Companies will be placing a greater emphasis on the quality of air and drinking water in the workplace as they shift to an emphasis on valuing their employees. Emissions of chemicals in fabrics, carpets, adhesives and other construction materials are detrimental to human health. The choice of these materials will be made more carefully with well-being in mind. Companies will also be pressuring suppliers to provide safe construction materials and stop producing materials that will harm the employee's health.

Air cleaners are being installed at more offices to purify the air. As awareness of the "sick building syndrome" has increased, growing numbers of companies are hiring contractors to periodically clean the air ducts to remove dust and debris that contain allergens, bacteria and viruses.

Many more areas stand out as places where firms can make a difference in their environmental impact. LEED (Leadership in Energy and Environmental Design) certification for constructing new buildings promises to reduce the footprint of corporate buildings. LEED standards, developed by the Green Building

Council, measure nine benchmarks, including sustainable site selection, contribution to air and water quality, recycled and reused materials, and sensitivity to regional issues (source: www. usgbc.org). Making such a commitment signals to customers that the company is serious about environmental issues and is not merely "green-washing," that is, making themselves appear to be ecologically-friendly without making any real changes.

The local and slow food movements are also changing business practices in agriculture and the restaurant industry. Shipping food over long distances increases the amount of greenhouse gases released into the atmosphere, and many consumers have begun buying locally to reduce this added impact. The definition of local can vary from buying vegetables from a farm in your county to one in the same region of the country. For the first time in decades, the number of farms in the United States has started increasing as part of this trend towards local food (source: USDA Census of Agriculture). Many of this produce is also grown organically, which reduces the amount of petroleum that goes into making fertilizer as well as the chemical runoff that leaches into streams and rivers. An added benefit goes to livestock, who are raised in a more humane manner on smaller farms.

The Native American tribe of the Lakota Indians had a saying— "Mi taku oyasin," which is translated as "we are all related", or "we are all connected." This universal message is at the core of our being. Everything is connected to everything. Everything has an impact on everything. Each action counts, and we must join hands to build a better world.

Chapter Twelve

Moving from Speed To Rhythm and Flow

> You work that you may keep pace with the earth and the soul of the earth.
>
> For to be idle is to become a stranger unto the seasons, and to step out of life's procession, that marches in majesty and proud submission towards the infinite.
>
> When you work you are a flute through whose heart the whispering of the hours turns to music.
>
> Kahlil Gibran
> *The Prophet*

Do it now. Do it fast. Even faster. The speed at which things are done is the weekly sermon that is preached aloud and silently in the workplace. A widespread belief that seems to prevail is that the success of a company depends on how quickly people move, and how fast processes deliver a product or service.

With the use of computers in the workplace and huge growth of the Internet, work can be accomplished more quickly. Information is much more readily available. And that information can allow us to make decisions more speedily.

Two key problems persist when speed becomes the focus:

1) <u>The standard for speed is always raised.</u> A young, bright accounting manager was hired by a sportswear manufacturer to work on the software system. Within six months, this young manager found several key areas that

needed changes, which reduced the time to close by half. In his recommendations to upper management, this manager also suggested that about half of the accounting staff was needed to operate this division.

While the results to the company were excellent, this posed a problem. When the young manager was promoted to another division, the bar of excellence was raised. The replacement in that divison was expected to perform at an even higher level. You can guess what happened. The new manager felt extreme pressure to perform at this higher level, and his performance was never fast enough. The result was burnout. Unfortunately, this highly qualified replacement left after six months, and the company missed an excellent opportunity with this new employee.

A very real risk with "speed" thinking is working under pressure, which stifles the creative process. As a result, some of the very best contributors leave the company.

2) <u>Mistakes can be made more easily.</u> A study was conducted to compare younger and older employees. The study showed conclusively that while younger employees could accomplish more, the number of errors were higher. On the other hand, older employees worked slower, but the number of mistakes were significantly less.

While this study may have something significant to say about the value of experience, I believe that it also points to the importance of working more carefully without the pressure of time.

Try this exercise. Think about the several key success stories in your company. Perhaps one was a new product introduction that experienced growth. Maybe it was a new manufacturing process that cut costs by a third.

Now identify the two or three primary events that were critical to each success story. What you will probably find are some common threads:

1) Effort was present, but struggle was absent.

2) Creativity was an important element.
3) The event was synchronous . . . it "just happened" naturally.

One night while sleeping, Isaac Singer had a vivid dream. He dreamed that a warrior was dancing with a spear, shaking it vigorously. The unusual thing about this spear is that the pointed end of the spear had a hole through it. Occasionally, the warrior would pierce a piece of cloth with his spear.

Upon awakening, Singer knew that he had dreamed up something innovative. It was the birth of the sewing machine, which has since made an enormous impact on the fabric and clothing industry across the globe.

Many of the success stories that eventually gave rise to prominent companies are similar to what happened to Singer. Perhaps it started in a dream. Or maybe someone stumbled onto something by accident.

The "80% rule" can be applied in a practical sense. The general rule of thumb states, "20% of your effort will yield 80% of the results." The idea is echoed by someone who once said, "focus on the majors . . . don't major on the minors." About 80% of your accomplishments will be achieved with little effort. The success stories will demonstrate that as well.

If speed, then, is not the answer to what we accomplish, what is?

I believe that the next paradigm to influence the corporate world will be the concept of rhythm. The idea behind rhythm is that the best way to accomplish is to fall into the natural rhythm of events.

Nature is about rhythm. The four seasons have its cycles. Like clockwork, the moon revolves around the earth every 28 days. The tide rises and falls in rhythm to the moon.

Following rhythm speaks of getting into the flow of life. While the concept sounds somewhat esoteric at first, its application is quite practical. The famous football quarterback, Joe Montana, has mentioned that he has noticed a common element in his most successful games. Prior to each game, Joe meditated to get into that still, quiet space. During the game, he observed that peak performance was achieved with ease. In fact, he described the process as though *he wasn't playing the game, rather the game was being played out through him.* Montana noticed that in subsequent games, the frequency for achieving remarkable plays increased with each game.

How do we therefore apply rhythm to the way we conduct business? It is through two concepts: Entrainment and cultivating a sense of timing.

Entrainment is nature's way of expressing rhythm. It is a phenomenon in nature that describes synchronous change. When a baby rests on a mother's breast, the baby's heartbeat falls into the same rhythm as its mother's heartbeat. Similarly, when several women live together for a length of time, their menstrual cycles begin to occur together. Entrainment is about allowing things to fall into the natural order of events. The logical mind might suggest calling a buyer immediately as the next step in closing a sale, but this might disrupt a natural rhythm that can only be known intuitively.

We prevent ourselves from getting into the flow by not accepting the reality that we experience. We move into the flow by surrendering to what the present moment offers, acknowledging the bigger picture and how we fit into it. By moving into the rhythm of the cosmos, we can stop working so hard to impose our plans.

Getting into rhythm requires less effort. It is essential to understand the difference between effort and struggle. Effort denotes the work that is invested in a project; struggle, on the other hand, implies negative emotion involved in the effort. That is, when one loses the awareness and works against the natural flow, the ego kicks in, striving so hard to achieve the objective.

Simply go with the flow, and there will be no struggle. When we resist that which we experience, struggle enters the scene. In nature, there is no struggle to achieve the most magnificent wonders on earth. In fact, usually little or no effort is involved. It simply is.

Another way to tell when we are out of the flow is when the joyfulness is absent. Joy is a naturally occurring feeling. Even excitement does not always involve joy. Excitement could result from a range of emotions.

Essentially, flow is the key to maximizing productivity at every level. Why? Because flow is about working with the universe. Setting goals and planning initiatives simply will not work if those strategies are out of touch with how nature and the rest of the universe is flowing. Simply put, getting into the flow is the way for producing results.

Jazz vibraphonist and educator Gary Burton described the process of getting into flow in an analogy to music. He said the following when asked about techniques he used to teach students to be spontaneous:

> "I tell them to use their ears instead of their brains. If I'm working with a student, I'll play something and tell them to play something back to me. Respond to it. React to it. Don't stop and study it. Answer it. Make musical conversation happen.
>
> Gradually what happens is that you let your unconscious mind make the decisions. This is the essential element for the jazz musician. When I'm playing, my mind has to make thousands of little decisions incredibly quickly. I couldn't possibly think about each one, consider each one, and make the decision. My unconscious mind can weigh all these alternative possibilities, pick the right one, time it exactly, coordinate the muscles, and make it happen.
>
> As I start to play a song, in those first few moments I step back from the process mentally, and the playing starts going on its own. I start watching it as if I'm an observer. The unconscious mind is now doing it. It's very natural for me now, after doing it for years. It wasn't so natural in my early days when I was much more conscious about my playing. But you learn to trust you unconscious mind."

At one point in my career, I was working with a Fortune 500 company that was difficult to work with in terms of getting the information that I needed internally. My objective was to map out the process for how that customer develops products. Picking up the phone and calling the customer contacts that I knew would have been a time-consuming process, and the information would have been incomplete.

One day, at the right time, I met someone outside of the company with whom I began to develop a close friendship. After several months, he casually mentioned that his brother worked with software. In a series of "coincidental" phone conversations, I found myself discussing business with his brother, and learned that he was hired by my customer to map out the process for how this customer engineered its products.

Bingo. I had access to all of the upper-level customers and gained an understanding of the process mapping. It worked out much more magnificently than what I or a team of people could have accomplished by developing a strategic plan for mapping out product creation at this Fortune 500 customer.

Some call that coincidental. Still others, lucky. I call it *synchronous* and going with the flow. I simply had the thought and let go of it, "allowing the universe" to bring it to fruition.

Deepak Chopra gives us the model for creation:

1) Have a desire.
2) Relinquish the attachment to the result.
3) Trust the universe to produce the results.

My good friend Alan Semonian has built a successful accounting practice. His clients love the speed at which he works, and they spread the word. Clients are in and out of his office in just a short time. He accomplishes more in a day than anyone I know. Why has he been so successful? Because Alan simply gets into the flow of what he does and *loves* it.

Remember that the universe can produce the results faster, simpler and with more ease than what you or I can try to do. It will bring into reality the object of your desires in the magical moment, the exact time for which it is perfection.

Chapter Thirteen

Taking Care of Your Employees' Concerns

A man there was, though some did count him mad,
The more he cast away, the more he had.

John Bunyan
The Pilgrim's Progress

Nearly every major company contains a similar statement in their employee handbook or in their mission statement:

"Employees are our greatest asset."

Yet, when looking at the reality of how those companies demonstrate this "value", the words don't carry any actual weight. Those companies spend little time determining what matters t to the employees and integrating the resources necessary to fulfill those concerns.

What would a company be like if performance appraisals were turned into a needs assessment session? I believe that a company would revolutionize its workforce by conducting these feedback sessions on an individual basis. The difficulty lies in creating a climate in which employees feel safe and valued enough to give an honest appraisal of their needs.

Establishing this approach begins by looking at how our society is changing. The number of single-parent families is growing. Also, the number of dual income families is growing. These facts point to the desperate need to provide on-site daycare services for employees. When companies demonstrate that they value the family, those organizations will be able to retain their employees, and most likely, the employees will be more excited about working for that company.

Companies that demonstrate concern for their employees will be most successful at hiring the best and retaining that talent. Consider James Goodnight and John Sall, the billionaires who started SAS (Statistical Analysis System), now the largest private software company in the United States. Located in North Carolina on hundreds of acres, SAS has a campus-like atmosphere, a day-care center, and a staff of full-time doctors. In a time of dual career families, this company has placed attention on fulfilling the needs of employees. Turnover is less than 4% a year, compared to 15% at the typical software firm in the U.S. (Forbes, October 14, 1996). Frisbee games can be seen on the lawns in the midst of lakes and manicured flower beds. SAS even sells plots of land to its employees at huge discounts to encourage them to take root close to the office. The company recognizes that its employees are much happier and more productive, while providing these nontaxable benefits.

The balance between work and home comes as a struggle for many professionals. Many companies often require employees to work on weekends, in addition to a normal work week. Moreover, some companies conduct mandatory meetings and seminars on Saturdays and Sundays, hacking away at the personal time of their employees.

While managers feel that they are maximizing the productivity of their employees by intruding on time of relaxation, the law of nature is forgotten. Rest is necessary; the time for rejuvenation must be taken. The body and mind will rebel. Science now tells us that the majority of "dis-ease" is a result of discomfort, in which we have not relaxed. Every expansion must follow with a relaxation. Life itself, and everything within it, flows in a cycle. Strain and stress occurs when this cycle is broken.

Another aspect of this law of nature is the law of giving and receiving. Asking more of employees, by asking them to sacrifice their personal time, for example, will be compensated by a loss somewhere else, in morale, creativity, or costs. True efficiency cannot be forced and results by getting into the natural harmony of the universe.

A company that is rising to the ranks of Fortune 500 status is approaching things differently. The CEO recently described the benefits of looking after employees:

"Management should be there to serve the people in a company. If they do that, then customer satisfaction happens."

Listen to the way that this CEO described the *people* in his company, not just as employees. Traditional companies tend to cultivate the opposite thinking in their organizational culture. Their prescription dictates that employees serve management's wishes and whims. If someone speaks out about other ideas, sometimes the giant corporate shoe descends down from the heavens and squashes that poor soul.

Chief Executive Ralph Horn of the First Tennessee National Bank heralds their success story. In his discussions with securities analysts, he emphasizes the link between loyal and committed employees and their satisfied customers. With no changes in staffing or systems, the loan volume has doubled at First Tennessee National with the fundamental change in its employee-friendly polices. And customer-service ratings have skyrocketed, from 38% good ratings in 1992 to 98%. (Wall Street Journal, Feb. or March 1997, front page of Marketplace).

Listen to the people in your company. Respect their opinions. Great ideas usually come from your people that are closest to the customer. Reward them for simply speaking their opinions. Take care of them, and customer satisfaction will happen.

Taking care of your employees is like taking care of your own physical body. We eat properly, exercise regularly, sleep the right amount, and so on. For many of us, our well-being is more important than making a lot of money. Nurture your "corporate" body as a top priority and it will deliver the results.

Take the mundane and make it exciting. Usually the "mundane" is important to your people. Consider the lunch hour. For companies like Oracle Corporation, noontime is more than a bologna sandwich with a soggy pickle. You might select seared ahi tuna or lemongrass teriyaki chicken served with pineapple chutney. Enjoy a cappacino at the coffee bar. Each item under $5 makes lunch exciting and affordable.

These companies understand the trends influencing the way we work and play. People are indulging in little pleasures, and that trend does not stop at the workplace. Businesses are also beginning to realize that taking care of employees leads to retaining quality talent. Creating excitement around the lunch hour is one way of easing the strain of long work schedules and maintaining a stronger focus by cycling between work and relaxation.

The rule is simple: Spend time and resources on your employees, and you will reap the rewards. Putting this rule into place requires courage, because it flies so much in the face of the conventional wisdom. The companies that truly take this rule to heart will position themselves in the vanguard of the next century.

A future trend that will occur in companies will be to develop a new position for a leader at a visible level in the organization. The role of this person will be to cultivate spiritual values throughout the company. While many companies will be tempted to integrate this function in their human resource activity, the importance of spirituality in an organization requires a strong focus. Providing that focus warrants a high-level staff position.

Companies now have leaders in quality, productivity, sales, and so forth. By adding a leader of "spirituality", it will send a strong signal throughout the company that will initiate awareness and establish importance.

Chapter Fourteen

Celebrating Diversity

> Conformity is one of the most fundamental dishonesties of all. When we reject our specialness, water down our God-given individuality and uniqueness, we begin to lose our freedom. The conformist is in no way a free man. He has to follow the herd.
>
> Norman Vincent Peale
> *Man, Morals and Maturity*

It is interesting to interview people and ask them about their perceptions of a company culture. More often than not, the adjectives that they use to describe the company also describe those who work there.

Most organizations have a culture that describes the types of individuals that belong to that organization, and how those people interface with the rest of the world. Some companies, for example, will be known for their aggressive sales force, while other companies will hire those with a softer sales approach, one that fosters building long-term relationships with customers.

Several years ago, the vice-president of human resources of a Fortune 500 company was giving a talk about the values of his company. He stressed that managers have been fired solely because they did not exhibit the values outlined in the corporate handbook. During the question and answer period, he was asked why the company hired these managers in the first place. His response was that the company occasionally makes mistakes.

Did the company act responsibly in placing these managers at high-level positions and firing them? It is doubtful that these managers suddenly changed their values overnight, leading them to the gallows. It was apparent that this corporation used their "company values" as an umbrella for moving people as they needed.

The corporate culture of a company is typically the result of the values of management, and how those values result in certain behaviors. Many companies, however, are discovering that they have created their own limitations by developing a culture made of individuals who fit their corporate mold and excluding those who fall out of the category with one or more characteristics: hair length, marital status, family status, music preference, etc.

Resourceful companies expand their thinking by hiring people who do not fill their traditional recipe. Those leaders are realizing that a more diverse company culture will be able to relate more directly to a diverse world.

Cultivating diversity in your organization is spiritually grounding. Observe those who exemplify spiritual values. Like attracts like. By whom do you want to be surrounded? Corporate management guru Tom Peters suggests to hang out with unusual people. They have exciting and innovative ideas. These types of people spawn ideas for the future. They are our creative leaders.

Diversity in an organization is about valuing each person and acknowledging the beauty that is present in each individual. Your people are the most important asset in your company. How you value those people and cultivate this ideology throughout the organization will ultimately determine your company's survival in today's culture.

Moving toward a more diverse culture in an organization is more than a spiritual issue. Legislation is certainly pushing us into that direction. In today's workplace, not embracing diversity has legal consequences. Companies as large as American Airlines or as small as a two-person convenience store are vulnerable to lawsuits by employees or former employees.

The US Equal Employment Opportunity Commission reported its highest ever number of charges in 2010, for offenses ranging from retaliation to equal compensation to racial discrimination. In addition to being illegal, such violations can lead to multimillion dollar penalties. Even if an offense is eventually deemed un-actionable, it still mars the reputation of the company as the dispute process makes its way through the courts. The most recent Wal-Mart discrimination case, now being heard by the Supreme Court will decide whether such cases can be brought as class actions (Source: The Guardian, Monday, March 28, 2011). Even if it loses the case, Wal-Mart will still be the world's largest retailer, but the blow to its reputation will remain and will one day spell disaster for this corporate giant.

The last decade has seen changes in civil rights legislation, including increasing action against discrimination based on sexual orientation and amendments to the Americans with Disabilities Act. Corporations can lead in this area, or they can be forced into compliance by the courts. Those companies that are seen as leaders will be better able to adapt to changes in society than those who are seen as behind the times. But beyond the numbers, companies should do the right thing simply because it is the right thing to do. Standing for equality makes for a better society, which ultimately benefits everyone.

If you have trouble accepting the fact that younger people throughout this planet are evolving into a universal culture, observe young people at school, in the coffee shops, and on the college campuses. Log onto Facebook. It will be evident that the youth are moving beyond tolerance, burgeoning into a world-wide culture that celebrates diversity in every way. Race, sex, religion, sexual orientation, and age do not matter. This is our destiny.

As our world continues to embrace true diversity, the walls that we have built to separate ourselves from one another are crumbling. At some point, there will be no need for reverse discrimination legislation or quotas.

Scott DeGarmo, editor of *Success* magazine, wrote of a fascinating piece about John Goode, a black restaurateur in Austin, Texas, who refused to be certified as a minority. In spite of losing a large contract with Austin's city convention center to supply food services, he did so because he believed he was no longer "disadvantaged." Goode explained, "I want to be judged on the quality of my food and the service that my staff and I provide. Why should I be forced to participate in set-asides or affirmative-action programs? In the free enterprise system, you need to be able to stand on your own and compete."

"I think minority businesses need to understand that a lot of times affirmative-action and set-aside programs do more to hurt than to help. Everyone looks at us as being incapable of doing the job," says Goode. He believes the minority youth are encouraged to not work as hard because they are "going to get a piece of it anyway."

This bold stand by John Goode is a shining example to anyone who considers themselves "handicapped" by society. To value integrity so highly in the face of risking the loss of revenue, the competitive edge, and significant business momentum is an encouraging sign that spiritual values are becoming paramount to a growing number of leaders. (Source: Success magazine, Jan./Feb. 1997, p. 4).

While women are being treated more equitably than before, the problem of unspoken sex discrimination remains. In 2010, only 15 of the Fortune 500 CEOs were women (Source CNN Money). The number declined to 12 in 2011. In 2010, men still dominated boardrooms, with 82% of the seats. In 2010, 27.4 % of Fortune 500 companies had no women in executive positions, including Exxon Mobil, Sears, and Costco. (source: Catalyst)

The National Association for Female Executives (NAFE) gives awards each year for companies with the best record for promoting women into top positions and for taking strides to reduce discrimination. Among those heading the list were Abbott (a healthcare company), American Express, Bank of America, and General Mills. These companies are all far from equitable, but they put programs in place to help women network and move up the corporate ladder. NAFE rewards them not on perfection but on making positive changes.

In 1989, Motorola began an aggressive initiative by looking at the census data. The objective of top management was to predict the future demographics of workers in the computer science and electrical engineering fields, and to set targets for its management structure to mirror the share of men, women, blacks, Asians, and other groups. As part of the succession planning process, top managers must name likely replacements, candidates for grooming, as well as the woman or minority that is closest to being qualified for that position. The managers are expected to provide experiences for the third category that will enable the individual to merit a promotion. Unknown to the candidates, the confidential process relieves pressure and helps avoid personnel conflicts.

Many women are leaving companies due to inequitable promotion practices, opting for smaller firms or even self-employment. Other women are evaluating corporate diversity practices and selecting those companies that encourage a culture of mutual respect and provide equal opportunities.

The key to evoking change in this area is to begin conversations with the women in your organization. Many companies believe that they understand the issues and desires of women. For example, in the initial discussions with the 80 female partners at Cooper and Lybrand, some of the senior members of the management committee, all of whom were male, assumed that the female partners did not want to travel. The women responded that they, in fact, wanted to meet clients in the field. The female partners also felt excluded from informal lunches. Another company uncovered a stereotypical misperception about women, assuming that they were not serious about their careers because of family commitments.

Age discrimination is one of the silent crimes that runs rampant through corporate America. Golden parachutes are the cloak for ridding companies of older employees.

One construction company received a wake-up call when a 56-year-old executive was forced to quit his job because of his age. When he sued the company, the jury awarded him $5.7 million.

What companies need to understand in the youth-oriented culture is that cutting costs should not be a reason to cut older employees. As this segment of the population continues to grow larger, we need to take advantage of the valuable experiences and resources that this group has to offer.

In cultivating diversity as a spiritual value, one of the issues I see companies struggling with is sexual orientation. While more companies are dealing with the issue openly and appropriately, many organizations still treat the subject as taboo in their diversity training. Many who do discuss diversity glaze the subject by focusing on including people with long hair, or those in a particular birth order.

The critical issues, however, must be dealt with in a straightforward approach. In a culture where a third of all teenage suicide result over issues dealing with sexual orientation, we desperately need to bring a halt to this tragedy, and to the problems of acceptance that occur in organizations among adults.

"Fred", who is an up and coming executive at a Fortune 500 company, was disturbed by a meeting he had several years ago with his manager. Explaining that he was "comfortable with diversity", his manager went on to ask him about how he entertains his clients, since "he didn't seem like one of the beer-drinking boys". Fred, who was on the fast track in his career, was shocked and troubled by his manager's innuendos. In short, his manager was dancing around the idea that he thought Fred was gay. In his next breath, his manager explained that Fred's coworkers "were not comfortable working with him."

This type of discussion was inappropriate. Not only did many of the manager's comments focus on a subject that has nothing to do with performance, it placed Fred in a very uncomfortable situation.

After this meeting, Fred sat down with each of his coworkers and separately asked them about his performance, what was he doing right, what could he be doing better, and if they were comfortable working with him. The employees were forthright, and their comments were positive in terms of Fred's performance.

Obviously, if the manager were truly comfortable with diversity, there would be no need for a discussion. The manager, uncomfortable with what he perceived to be Fred's sexual orientation, wanted to see how Fred would react. The fascinating part of this story is that this large corporation spends a lot of money on diversity development for managers, but does not appear to grasp the entire meaning around the issues.

In many organizations, insecure managers need power in order to prevent exposure of a personal sense of inadequacy. Feeling out of control, managers lacking in self-worth project power as a compensation for an inner imbalance. By having knowledge of some attribute or weakness of an employee, a manager may opt to use that knowledge to feel "empowered", as the use of the knowledge will temporarily make him appear stronger, and his employee feel weaker. These ego trips driven by incomplete managers will disappear as companies create "inner workshops". Once managers have a legitimate outlet to air their feelings of inadequacy, they will no longer need to use vulgar displays of power.

Honoring diversity leaves no room for prejudice. Respecting differences knows no hate or separation. Celebrating diversity in its truest sense is about unconditional love. And love transcends color, religion, cultural differences, ethnic heritage, and sexual orientation.

A recent program on a popular talk show featured a hermaphrodite, a person who is born with the sexual organs of both a man and a woman. This person openly discussed the challenges of growing up in a world of prejudice and cruelty. In spite of having a deeper voice and larger hands, this person developed breasts and took on the role of a woman. Classmates at school would taunt this person, making horrible jokes about being a man.

The question that arose while watching this program was, "How would I want to be treated if I were born under such circumstances?" Ask yourself the question and imagine that your organization employed a hermaphrodite. Or imagine that you were that person in your organization. How would you want the organization to deal with this issue? How would you want to be treated? The answer will lead you to consider how your corporate culture might evolve to embrace diversity of any sort.

The original film *The Elephant Man* brought tears to my eyes at the peak of the movie, in the moment during which this disfigured man was being physically abused by the crowd. In his moment of desperation, the elephant man mustered all of the strength in his voice and cried out, "I am a human being!" What a moment of awakening. If only we could see each other as human beings who are crying out to simply be loved, rather than to see our differences.

Companies that continue to cultivate a particular type of "culture" based on physical attributes are thinking with limitations. A truly boundary-less company has no need for diversity training, as it attracts employees who are diverse and honor it. But as long as prejudice and separatist thinking exists, the need for proactively cultivating a culture of diversity will be necessary.

The successful company will be one that has no particular identity. It will flow with the ideas from relaxed, free people from every walk of life. That organization will be "color-blind", and will be blind to other things that have long separated us from one another.

Internal reviews to support ethnic quotas will be a thing of the past. The need for policy becomes necessary when an imbalance exists. When our society no longer evaluates based on sex, race, or any other type of discriminated category, policy, legislation and conflict will become a thing of the past. As the individuals in our society continue to evolve toward wholeness, prejudice melts away.

Chapter Fifteen

The New Paradigm for Leadership

The vocation of every man and woman is to serve other people.

Leo Tolstoy
War and Peace

The leaders in the organizational structure must manifest their spirituality to allow it to flow throughout the organization.

Traditional organizations typically promote people into leadership positions based upon performance or the ability to get things done. The change that is beginning to take place is that some organizations are recognizing the importance of aligning the direction of the organization with spiritual values. They are realizing that the least amount of struggle, or flow, occurs when the organization is aligned with the flow of the universe, from which arises spiritual values.

Mort Meyerson, Chairman of Perot Systems, recently said the following about what it means to lead:

> Learn the difference between direct and indirect leadership, and then apply it to yourself. Most companies are still dominated by numbers, information, and analysis. That makes it much harder to tap into intuition, feelings, and nonlinear thinking—the skills that leaders will need to succeed in the future.
>
> Which of these two messages do you think motivates a team more effectively: *Case 1*: "Here is the year's profit-and-loss objective. If we make our numbers, you will get your

bonus at the end of the year, with stock-options vesting in three years. Oh by the way, we believe people are our most important asset." *Case 2*: "Here is our philosophy: Take care of your customer. Take care of your fellow team members. Then tangible results will follow."

I think the answer is obvious. The first approach will work well in the short term, but the team will not feel better for having done it. The second approach is sustainable, can be scaled up to include large numbers of people, and the team will feel better about its performance. If you work with the whole person, and their whole mind, you will reach a better place, for them and the company." (Source: Fast Company, Feb./Mar 1997, p.99)

The organizations that will be most successful will be those that promote leaders based primarily on exhibiting spiritual values. The sign of a leader will be how connected he or she is. "In spirit", or inspiration, will be the lifeblood of an employee.

Forward-looking companies today have taken the roles formerly held by middle managers and dispersed the leadership responsibilities among numerous employees. Job descriptions have become loose, flexible descriptors rather than contractual commitments. As job titles become less and less meaningful, the burden of responsibility widens to encompass every member of the firm.

On the individual level, volunteering is an excellent teacher, exposing us to an environment of equality. In volunteer organizations, there is no status. Volunteering is effective, as it strips away power. Everyone is equal, seeking to create a better world in a unified effort. Volunteering will change your perspective of hierarchy and authority.

Some organizations are encouraging their employees to get involved in volunteering positions with the American Red Cross, for example, who assists with local disasters in the community. Still others get involved in a community effort such as Meals-on-Wheels, whose dedicated focus is to deliver meals to homebound seniors. The commitment to time is often insignificant, requiring only a minimum of 4-6 hours per month. But the impact it has on the people that are touched by this is immeasurable.

Skandia, the $7 billion insurance giant in Sweden, has established an important precedence for setting the strategic direction of their company. A top leader in their company, Leif Edvinsson, selected a group of 30 people around the globe to form Future Teams, as part of the Skandia Future Centers (SFC). Their mission was to develop a vision of the future for the company.

Based on a "3G" model, a mix of three generations ranging from the 20s to the 60s, and diverse backgrounds, experiences and functions, the group is poised to continually redefine its future. "We want to make the organization more transparent and thus reduce the lead time from learning to teaching," says Edvinsson.

He has included younger people in the development of strategy, a practice that is quite uncommon in North American corporate culture. Edvinsson says, "We need people who can understand the archeology of the future. That's why we have these 25-year olds in our program. They already have that vision—they carry the icons of tomorrow with them." (Source: Fast Company, January/February 1997 issue, p. 58).

A challenge for all organizations, including corporations, stores, churches, and museums, would be to develop a diverse group of leaders, irrespective of tenure or age. The results will probably be surprising. Toy companies could include 5-year-olds to sit on the board. What do 60-year-old board members who are running a trucking company know about making toys?

Leadership is also about listening to the people in your company, find out what they like to do, and let them do it. Unleashing them where they are motivated is powerful. Consider how our bodies work. Groups of cells are organized in tissues, and tissues combine to perform a function as organs. A heart cell is different from a liver cell. You wouldn't place a heart cell in a liver and expect the heart cell to function in concert with the rest of the liver cells. Similarly, strive to identify which "cells" in your organizational body perform certain functions, and organize them accordingly.

Try placing kidney tissue in a bone, and see how long it takes for both to function in disharmony.

Jack Welch, one of the most respected CEOs, said the following about leadership, as quoted in Fortune magazine on March 26, 1990:

> "We have to undo a 100-year-old concept and convince
> our managers that their role is not to control people and stay
> 'on top' of things, but rather to guide, energize, and excite."

Organizations need fewer *managers of people*. People do not need to be managed. Processes need to be managed. Managing processes is about continuously re-engineering the way we operate.

Managing people is simply a function of control, the primary goal of the ego. To relinquish control, however, is the ultimate place of power and the seat of change. Bill Gross founded Idealab, a company that generates ideas and turns them into successful businesses. Gross, who has created over 19 companies, said the following about how he allows companies to develop: I can run around like a hummingbird, plugging my ideas into multiple, highly focused companies. For me the clincher was this: I have ideas all the time. My satisfaction is gauged by the percentage of them that turn into reality. I found that by relinquishing control, a higher net percentage of what I visualize in my brain is seeing the light of day."

This new paradigm is contrary to how we have traditionally believed results are produced. The recipe used to include sticking with one idea, careful management, and driving home that idea to fruition.

The process for hiring is evolving. Rather than to promote or hire people based on analytical thinking, practice going with your "gut" instincts. The mind, as it has experienced fear and doubt, will usually throw in those elements during analysis. The gut, on the other hand, has not learned to doubt. Trust it. Practice sensing those feelings. Ask questions internally, and wait for that response from your "gut." There is a higher purpose in hiring those whom you feel strongly about hiring, or those to whom you are drawn, even though it does not make logical sense to those around you.

As you practice trusting yourself for the answers, your body will respond and will always be correct. Why is this? It is because "you" are non-local and are connected to the universe.

Chapter Sixteen

Focus on the Individual

The whole point of this life is the healing of the heart's eye through which God is seen.

St. Augustine of Hippo

Why do companies today spend so much time on team-building? This concept is based on fear. Managers often seem afraid of not accomplishing a task, especially if they believe that it is because people won't cooperate as a result of intrapersonal conflict.

So the managers set up team-building exercises. Lots of ice-breakers.

Companies would be better off if interviews were focused more on inner work, rather than a resume filled with lots of experience at lots of places and a long list of accomplishments.

Some of those questions in an interview setting might be the following:

1) How would you describe your spiritual journey?
2) What kind of inner work have you done in the past two years?
3) We offer many inner workshops. What areas would you like to work on with us supporting you?
4) What is it that you love to do and why?

It was disappointing to hear a president of a large company recently tell its leaders to get rid of the low performers, and to concentrate on developing the better performers. The problem with this philosophy is that even if the company got rid of the worst performers, that company would always have people "at the bottom" considered poor performers. This attitude cultivates an environment of fear, in which the employees are concerned with ratings and evaluations.

As we progress, organizations will emphasize development of the individual, rather than to abandon the individual. Studies have shown that quite often poor performance is a function of a problematic process, not of the individual. Again, attention to the process is important.

The need to evaluate employees will become less important. In these cases, evaluation is a function of judgment and analysis.

In *Hamlet*, William Shakespeare wrote, "There is nothing either good or bad, but thinking makes it so." So much of our upbringing, however, teaches us to think in terms of what is good, bad, right or wrong. This vicious cycle of analysis is a violent action of the mind. Dr. Wayne Dyer has described analysis as a process involving tearing something apart, and synthesis as putting something together.

Cultivate skills in your employees that transcend time. Let go of catch phrases that are ego-based. Often such transient phrases are faddish in nature, employed by someone who wants to make his or her mark for advancement. Instead cultivate those values that are spiritually based:

- Self-love
- Serving others, selflessness
- Universal thinking—we are all connected
- Peace
- Compassion
- Tolerance

The new training frontier will be focused on inner work of individuals. We are learning that people are bringing their dysfunctional behaviors into the workplace. These behaviors are usually the result of being wounded as a child. Studies in England and the United States have shown that 50 to 75 percent of all problems of people attending primary care clinics are emotional, social, or familial in origin, even though those issues are being expressed by pain or illness. (Source: Rosen, G.; Kleinman, A.; and

Katon, W. "Somatization in Family Practice: A Biopsychosocial Approah." *Journal of Family Practice* 14 no. 3 (Mar 1982): 493-502.—and—Stoeckle, J.D.; Zola, I.K.; and Davidson, G.E. "The Quantity and Significance of Psychological Distress in Medical Patients: Some Preliminary Observations about the Decision to Seek Medical Aid." *Journal of Chronic Disease* 17 (Oct 1964): 959-970.)

As companies begin to devote resources to inner work, individuals will become whole. Productivity will increase. Harmony will fill the environment. Employees will be happier. And loyalty to the company will rise, which will be an important competitive advantage.

Inner work gets to the heart of issues. In the West, medicine and therapies tend to focus on symptoms. People reach for the aspirin when they have headache. But the aspirin does not relieve the cause of the headache; rather, the aspirin relieves the headache, which is the effect.

Inner work tends to have its roots based on principles that are shared with Eastern tradition and medicine. The therapies go beyond the result, or the effect, of the imbalance and work to bring the system back into balance.

Some of the suggested practices for inner work that are being incorporated into the workplace are outlined below. While some leaders have difficulty imagining having "therapies" incorporated into their wellness programs, the integration of these types of inner work will be commonplace.

Yoga

Based on the wisdom of the East, yoga has been associated with reducing stress for many people. Yoga incorporates physical postures, meditation and breathing exercises that have a healing and relaxing effect on the mind, body and spirit. The body's own inner wisdom can be unlocked by understanding the interconnections between the physical body, the mind, emotions, breath and energy movement.

Thousands of studies have been conducted since the early 1970s that demonstrate the effectiveness of yoga in reducing stress and anxiety, heightening auditory and visual perception, and improving intelligence and memory. The benefits of providing yoga classes at 7:30 every morning, for example, will be realized in the workplace.

Guided Imagery

A very common technique for relaxation, guided imagery is used to reduce susceptibility to disease, controlling pain, reducing anxiety and depression, and alleviating stress.

Guided imagery is also conducted in creativity sessions in the workplace to provide an environment for producing ideas. This technique is helpful for strengthening the imagination and ability to develop mental pictures.

Bodywork

Every time we experience an emotion, the body produces chemicals that are stored in the muscle and fat tissues. Essentially, the physical body becomes a storehouse for memories. When the body is touched at a location of these stored molecules, the emotional chemistry is released, and the person often experiences the memory associated with the emotions involved.

Many forms of bodywork have been used for centuries, from therapeutic massage to deep tissue therapies such as Hellerwork and Rolfing®. Energetic forms of bodywork include polarity therapy and acupressure. It will not be long before companies regularly hire polarity energy practitioners and pranic healers to work with employees to bring the energy in the body into balance.

Bodywork has demonstrated how the mind, emotions and physical body are interconnected. Foot reflexology, for example, is a well-known and accepted form of how the parts of the body are related to the foot. But energy is reflected in numerous ways throughout the body, linking members to other members of the body. The emotional and spiritual elements of an individual can be accessed as well through various techniques to bring about balance and wellness.

Great companies will set up meditation sites in their company. Already, many companies in the East follow this tradition. In the

United States, some sports teams have regular meditation sessions during training and prior to games.

Deepak Chopra, best-selling author of *The Seven Spiritual Laws of Success* and *Ageless Body, Timeless Mind*, once said, "If you were to ask me what was the most significant experience of my life, I would say it was learning to meditate. For me that is the most important thing a person can do to restore harmony and evolve to a higher state of consciousness."

These practices will allow movement toward greater degrees of freedom and functionality. As smaller units in an organization are made whole, the organization becomes whole. Subsequently, as an individual is healed, the organization functions better.

The rate at which a company invests in healing, the more progress the company will make. Inner work will lead to mobilization.

Chapter Seventeen

Creating Magic in the Moment

"The good thing about the future is that it comes one day at a time."

Abraham Lincoln

The past and future do not exist. In his award-winning book **The Dancing Wu Li Masters**, Gary Zukav brilliantly discussed how the illusion of time is dependent on the observer, and does not exist in absolute form. In the last twenty-five years, quantum physics has demonstrated that all of time is bundled into the present moment. The illusion is that we are led to believe that just five minutes ago, we were reading the previous page. And yesterday, we mowed the lawn. Each moment leads into the next. But we remain ever present in the "now" moment.

Successful companies today are learning to spend less time "establishing goals" and thinking about what they want to accomplish tomorrow. Dwell on today. Tomorrow will take care of itself.

Living in the present moment means to live consciously. More people are learning to eat consciously, to savor the food, experiencing each bite and tasting the flavors.

What thoughts are you having in the present moment? What intuitions or insights are rising up in your consciousness? As we become more aware of our thoughts and focus intently upon the present moment, we will produce "real magic." The mechanics of creation exist while focusing on the only reality . . . now.

What is your body telling you? Your body is your extended environment and extended mind. It accurately projects the thoughts and emotions that you have covered up and that are seeking to be released. The inner work is the process that allows this release to happen.

Learn to trust your body and the messages that it sends. Our western culture has cultivated the habit of relying too heavily on *logos*, our logic, and less on *emos*, the emotional and creative part of us. Practice sensing your body and its reactions. The majority of your "effort" should be in listening . . . listening to your body, your senses, your environment, and the people in it.

Cultivate your body. It is the temple of God. Take care of it. Feed and nourish it properly. Get the right amount of rest. Your body is one of your best feedback mechanisms. The body is connected in an unlimited number of ways, which is demonstrated in the science of reflexology. Your physical body is also connected to the deeper parts of you . . . your subconscious, your soul.

Practice listening to your body when making important decisions. After a while of trusting, you will learn to sense those signals that will guide you to do the proper thing.

Chapter Eighteen

Managing Information

For knowledge itself is power.

Francis Bacon
Religious Meditations

The key to any company's success is how they process information, both internally and externally. How a company manages its information will be essential to its long-term growth and health.

Information is fast becoming the central focus of our business leaders. The ability to leverage information will determine the competitive advantage and well-being of an organization. While it is probably the most important commodity of any business, the systems that process information are becoming less expensive. But "less expensive" does not mean that communication becomes more effective, and this is where some strategic thinking is beneficial.

There are three primary areas of managing information that can be applied to probably any organization.

1) Internal processes (manufacturing, accounting, etc.)
2) Pulling information into the company from outside (e.g. customers, suppliers, research)
3) Supplying information to the outside (e.g. customers, suppliers)

Graphically, this process can be represented by the following diagram:

To revolutionize your company, begin a process what I call information flow mapping (IFM). IFM will involve examining these three areas in detail.

How does a company embark on the IFM process? Basically, you can approach this process from two ways: 1) Map out the current process. or 2) Start fresh and map out the process as simply as it can be. However you do this, the final result should indicate a process that is as simple as it can be.

When the information flow is mapped, you will discover several things:

1) All information is linked.
2) Each piece of information is dependent on all of the other pieces.
3) Much information gathering can be automated.

After mapping out the flow of information, it will become apparent which areas in the organization need adjustment and which tools are needed to serve the new flow process.

When the information process is mapped, the data can be grouped into "fields". The output of this process will resemble database architecture, with formats, fields and links. The system that needs to be developed around the IFM process will naturally emerge, as the input and output variables are defined. How each area is linked will also become apparent.

Who should create the information flow mapping? I suggest using your current organization. The people who best know these processes are those who live in them daily. They will be knowledgeable about the internal processes, market research, customer input, accounts receivable, and accounts payable.

Building quality into the products and services of your organization will be one of the most important benefits of IFM. Quality is a function of consistency in action, and developing processes around how information flows is at the heart of consistency.

The first step in managing information flow will be to put information systems, such as computer networks, into place. Beyond the traditional forms of systems, the information technology that will become the leading technology is *meditation*. While this sounds far-fetched to many, people who meditate are learning that one powerful result of this practice is that intuition dramatically increases. One feels more connected as meditation is practiced. This best technology also costs nothing.

Meditation allows us to be connected to "the Source." It is the most effective tool to get at the three areas of managing information. Getting connected to "the Source" means getting connected to the ultimate database. The regular practice of meditation makes the Internet look like an abridged dictionary containing only 500 words.

Chapter Nineteen

Awakening to Quality of Life

> We can make up our minds whether our lives in this world shall wound like thorns and nettles, or be beautiful and fragrant like the lilies of the field.
>
> Friar Andrew SDC
> *Meditations for Every Day*

The president of a successful company that is quickly rising to the ranks of Fortune 500 status recently discussed quality at a conference. He said, "Our quality process is not only making defect-free products. It is development, innovation, and quality of work life. It is about expanding capabilities. Safety has a lot to do with quality. For our company, safety is first, then quality. We take a personal interest in the well-being of our people. What are you doing to change the human system?" He later went on to say that "over-control is the disease of American management."

The common thread woven throughout his discussion was about delving into the souls of the people in an organization. Respecting their issues, listening to their concerns, and taking care of their needs in a very real way. Hire the best people and bring out the best in them. The result will be quality people delivering quality products and services for quality customers. At the heart of this process will be an awakening . . . an awakening to a quality of life.

Developing a quality of life in the workplace is become an urgent matter, as costs relating to worker safety continue to rise. A new survey reveals that costs related to cumulative trauma disorders (CTDs) are the fourth higher concern among U.S.

executives responsible for protecting corporate assets. (Source: CTD News online, Center for Workplace Health Information). It is estimated that American employers spend more than $7.4 billion a year in workers compensations and considerably more on medical treatment and hidden costs.

Rising costs also come from increasing litigation. The California Workers' Compensation Institute, a nonprofit organization, found employers paid 33 cents in litigation costs for every dollar paid in benefits for cumulative injury cases, while only 15 cents for every dollar of incurred benefits for other injury claims.

A common attitude among workers exhibits a certain degree of selfishness: "I got hurt. Now, you (the employer) fix me." To face this issue, companies must teach responsibility, but balance the education by providing a safer work environment.

Alarming many companies, these statistics have led to a focus on ergonomics, producing some impressive results. Companies are hiring ergonomists to teach employees ways to analyze jobs and develop ideas for improvement. With some training, individuals come up with solutions that are often inexpensive or cost nothing at all.

Ergonomics have arisen out of the problem. Proactively developing improvements in the workplace that come from true concern for the employee, and not just to cut rising costs, will be the trend. What is productivity in terms of reducing variable cost or increasing the number of widgets per hour if it does not lead to a better world? The planet is littered with the living skeletons of companies whose managers focus on bottom-line results, while the people feel empty, ignored and unfulfilled.

Think about the products we deliver. Organizations are not manufacturing widgets, selling groceries or providing financial services. We are "manufacturing" *love*, and delivering that love to those around us. If we are to deliver the maximum benefit to our customers, we want that love infused into our products and services by the people who touch them. This is precisely why a primary focus on the people in an organization will deliver more value to customers.

Gateway, a leading manufacturer of computer systems, has recognized the power of integrating the essence of spirit into each part they assemble. Jim Taylor, senior vice president for global marketing at Gateway, had the following to say:

> "There's no difference between what we sell and who we are. The Gateway brand is really just the aggregate personality of the people who work here. We have more than 9,000 employees. Each of them has 7 close friends; each of those friends has 7 friends. That's more than 440,000 people—and they all have email! We can't market a lie. We have to be cow-spotted everywhere, from how we build our machines to how we treat our people.
>
> Most of what's wrong with advertising would go away if companies understood that the first job of an ad is not to create a one-way communication with customers, but to enact conversations inside the company. At Gateway, advertising is a communication from the company to the company—*we talk to ourselves first*. That means we often advertise in media we know our own people read over media that we know they don't read, even if other media might deliver a better audience.
>
> You won't believe the reaction when we run an ad that doesn't feel "Gateway." We get thousands of emails from our people. That means our employees become the customer's best friend. They won't let us lie or shade the truth; they'd get wildly insulted." (Source: Fast Company, Jan/Feb 97, p. 85)

How do your employees feel about your company? If you get at the heart of this question, you will find a strong correlation between how your employees feel about your company, and how your customers feel about your company. Your customers will sense that feeling in your employees, your products, your services, your quality . . . in everything that they do. Customers will ultimately sense the "reality." This is the power of spirit.

Improving quality is much more than a cheerleading session. Dr. W. Edwards Deming emphasized the elimination of slogans, exhortations, and targets for the work force asking for zero defects and new levels of productivity. He believed that such "rah-rah" slogans only created adversarial relationships, as the majority of the causes of low productivity and poor quality belong to the system and therefore are beyond the power of the work team. Yet, many production plants are filled with signs that say "Zero Defects," or "Quality is about everything we do."

Real inclusion changes the way we think about quality. A fast-growing company formed its board of directors with team members, rather than the typical structure of CEOs of outside companies, the network of "friends" patting each other on the back. This company preaches "liberation management" and continually seeks out ways to liberate its people. A board of directors constructed from team members sends an unwavering message to the world: "We value our people . . . they are truly our strongest assets . . . this is the way we deliver quality to our customers."

Quality is truly a differentiating factor in business. Undoubtedly, it is imperative that a strong emphasis should be made on the quality of products and services delivered to the customer. But what traditional thinking companies do is focus on delivering quality products and services, and forget about the people. Building a culture around the quality of life is at the very center of spiritual values. Do this, and you will also witness the benefits of building a culture of *employee satisfaction* and customer satisfaction.

Chapter Twenty

The Birth of a New Workplace

You cannot teach a man anything. You can only help him
to find it within himself.

Galileo

The evolution of the workplace has already begun. Companies
across the globe are awakening to the importance of focusing
on the individual, and developing specialized internal "products
and services" to serve each person. By healing each person, the
whole becomes not just *incrementally* healed by that much, but
exponentially. A single kernel of corn planted in the ground and
cultivated with care grows into a beautiful stalk, yielding its fruit
of several ears of corn, each containing hundreds of corn kernels.
All of life reflects this law of nature.

Ignoring people, the very core of our workplace, is costly. The
Occupational Health and Safety News and the National Council
on Compensation Insurance reports that stress accounts for
$26 billion in medical and disability payments and $95 billion in
productivity loss. Stress also keeps about one million people a
day from going to work and causes one third of American workers
to seriously consider quitting their jobs. The cost is high: 85% of
employee accidents and 75% of reported high frequency illness in
employees are stress-related.

Can companies afford to continue being part of these statistics? The
savings to companies and their employees can be realized if attention
is placed on relieving stress. The following is a series of suggested
practices that encompass a wide range of therapies. Many companies
worldwide have witnessed the positive results of these practices.

Massage Therapy

Massage therapy has been perceived traditionally as a luxury, or as a way to pamper someone. Today, however, massage therapy has been proven to be an effective tool used to increase productivity and reduce stress in the workplace. Many companies are including on-site massage as part of a successful wellness program.

On-site massage is convenient for the employee, as the therapist uses a seated massage. No sheets or oils are used, and the massage takes place directly through the clothing. The workday is not disrupted, as an effective treatment usually takes about fifteen to twenty minutes.

The benefits from a therapist's touch are many. The massage will loosen tense muscles and stimulate circulation. The ability to think and concentrate will be enhanced as the circulation of oxygen-rich blood increases. The massage will also alleviate some of the pain of chronic job-related conditions, such as carpal tunnel syndrome.

Aqua-Gulf, a transportation and logistics company located in Deerfield Beach, Florida, contracted a leading therapeutic massage practice based in Boca Raton to provide on-site massage every week for employees. The corporation subsidizes 75% of the cost of the treatment. Aqua-Gulf's upper management believes that healthy employees result in increased productivity and enhanced customer satisfaction. Its employees have commented that the sessions provide a significant reduction in the job stress that can be part of the freight and logistics business.

John Bruno, President of Aqua-Gulf, stated, "After my short massage sessions, I'm able to return to my desk, rejuvenated and with a fresh perspective on various problems and issues." The company believes that employee morale is boosted and the company has a competitive advantage with happier employees, better service, and more satisfied customers.

CIGNA Corporation, in Hartford, Connecticut, has offered massage as part of the company's local medical program for the last two years. Finding the therapy to be an effective way for energize its employees, it offers sessions of 15 minutes to an hour.

Meditation

Some studies suggest that about 60-90% of visits to healthcare professionals are for stress-related conditions. Health problems, such as heart disease and ulcers, are now believed to be stress-related. Two fundamental changes happen that result in these diseases: the chemical changes in the body, and the fundamental change in breathing.

An effective technique that was has been practiced in the East for centuries can bring balance back into these functions. Through meditation, the breathing can become natural, and the body chemistry can return to normalized levels, even reversing conditions such as heart disease.

One form of meditation, transcendental meditation, has been studied at 210 universities and research institutions in 27 countries. Over four million people practice transcendental meditation all over the world and have discovered the proven benefits that have discussed in articles of more than 100 scientific journals:

1. Improved health: Reduced stress and anxiety, reduced hospitalization, reduced incidence of disease, reduced need for out-patient medical care, reduced healthcare costs, reduced use of alcohol and drugs, improved cardiovascular health, reduced physical complaints, increased longevity.

2. Improved mental abilities: Increased intelligence, increased creativity, improved learning ability and memory, faster reaction time, higher levels of moral reasoning, excelled academic achievement, greater orderliness of brain functioning, increased self-actualization.

3. Improved social behavior: Higher self-confidence, less anxiety, improved family life, improved relationships at home and at work, increased tolerance, improved job performance, and better job satisfaction.

The Transcendental Meditation technique is simple, nature and effortless. During this 15-20 minute procedure, the individual sits comfortably with the eyes closed preferably in a quiet room. Gradually, the awareness settles down into a state of restful alertness, distinct from the other states of waking, dreaming, and deep sleep.

The American Heart Association published in August 5, 1996, results in its journal Hypertension, showing that "the TM technique significantly lowered blood pressure in older African-American men and women who were at risk for five major risk factor groups." The American Journal of Managed Care conducted a study in 1996 that a TM program can result in savings of up to 75 percent of the cost of anti-hypertension drugs.

Aromatherapy

Aromatherapy began as an ancient art that is traced to Egypt 5000 years ago. Scientific research confirms the ability of essential oils extracted from plants and herbs to influence our moods and emotions, and to stimulate or relax the biological systems of the body. Essential oils are used widely throughout Europe, including England, where hospital nursing staffs administer oil massage to relieve pain and induce sleep. In France, physicians routinely prescribe aromatherapy preparations, recognizing the benefits in alleviating stress. Vaporized essential oils, such as lavender and lemon, are used to help combat the transmission of airborne infectious diseases.

The power of scent works as aromatic molecules interact with the nasal cavity, were signals are sent from the olfactory bulb, thereby stimulating the limbic brain, the emotional switchboard. The limbic system is directly connected to the parts of the brain that control the primary functions of the body, including heart rate, breathing, blood pressure, stress levels, memory and hormone levels. Because of the direct connection, some scientists believe that oil fragrances are one of the fastest ways to achieve physiological and psychological effects.

The essences of flowers and plants can be used in massage, in a gargle, in a hot bath, in a spray, or even internally, depending on the oil. The use of aromatherapy will permeate the workplace, as companies begin to develop "mood rooms". One room may be for relaxation, another for energizing and increasing alertness. I envision units that are installed in the ventilation systems that release aromas at levels too subtle to be consciously detected, but have a significant impact on productivity. The amount of time needed to complete a visual search task or rank a set of information can be cut in half by using essential oils.

The balance between inducing productivity and relaxation is necessary to achieve peak performance. The body and mind must experience moments of relaxation throughout the day. These special rooms can help facilitate the cyclical changes needed. For example, one might rest for five minutes in a blue room filled with lavender scent before walking into a creativity session where the air is permeated with peppermint. The blue colors and lavender odor will clear the mind, preparing it for a stimulating creativity meeting that is enhanced with the energizing scent of peppermint. Ideas will flow like water.

To create the "mood rooms" or to begin using aromatherapy in the workplace with misters or diffusers, the following is an abbreviated listing of more commonly used essential oils and their corresponding effects:

Essential Oils	Physiological and Psychological Effect
Lavender	Inner balance, peace, and calm
Sandalwood, fir	Relaxation, moving inward
Peppermint	Energizing
Basil	Relieves headaches; brings clarity
Rosemary	Greater mental alertness and memory
Eucalyptus, pine	Tranquility; opens lungs and clears respiration
Lime	Uplifts mental apathy and depression
Geranium	Regulates endocrine system; lifts spirits
Chamomile	Relives insomnia and irritability
Cinnamon, ginger	Stimulates clogged digestive system
Thyme	Strengthens immune system
Cedarwood	Opens lungs and relieves asthma
Cypress	Balances dry coughs and congestion

Colors

The use of color has been found to be an important element in affecting our moods and the way we think and behave. According to Maria Simpson, Director of the Health, Weight, and Stress Clinic at Johns Hopkins Medical Institutions, many restaurants and fast-food places decorate their dining rooms in orange, yellow and red, as bright colors have been found to increase the appetite.

For many years, McDonald's has incorporated bright red and yellow in its logo, signs, and restaurant decor. This colorful imagery is exciting and happy, resulting from not only the messages in the advertising and characters, but also the actual colors used throughout the stores. These colors evoke cheerful eating experiences that are powerful and promote customer loyalty, as these emotions are triggered repeatedly by dining under the golden arches.

In 1942, the Russian scientist S. V. Krakov conducted experiments that demonstrated how certain colors stimulate hormone production, while other colors inhibit it. He also proved that red light stimulates the sympathetic nervous system, while white and blue light stimulate the parasympathetic nervous system. (Source: Alternative Medicine, p.325) In the earlier part of the century, it was discovered that the symptoms of smallpox and measles were relieved when patients were put in a room with red windows.

Bright flashing lights are also used to treat pain and depression. Violet light, for example, has been used to induce relaxation, reduce stress and ease chronic pain. Photo-stimulation causes the brain waves to synchronize, resulting in these powerful physiological changes.

The color blue has been known to induce tranquility. Rooms painted with a blue color can be an effective means to create a space for relaxation. Or perhaps a mural of a blue ocean could be painted on a wall to achieve this mood.

Companies will begin shedding the traditional drab "cube-dominiums", and allow their people to decorate their workspace as they want. Most people will probably not opt for the ever popular earth tones with shades of gray, taupe or beige. The workplace will be alive and vibrant, filled with personal touches that will allow creative ideas to bubble up and productivity to soar.

Sound

Sound has been used for thousands of years as an effective treatment to reduce stress, alleviate pain, promote strength and endurance, improve movement, and increase intelligence. The power of sound can be demonstrated with music, which causes dynamic changes in the physiology.

A recent study conducted by two psychology professors at Wilkes University in Wilkes-Barre, Pennsylvania, demonstrated that certain types of music stimulate the body to produce an antibody called Immunoglobulin A. Although the work is preliminary, the study was conducted with Muzak Inc., a Seattle company that supplies background music to relieve workplace stress. (Wall Street Journal, Mar. 27, 1997, p. A1).

More companies are playing soft music in the lobbies and throughout the corridors to promote relaxation. Other organizations will be using sound therapy with biofeedback instruments to reduce stress. The use of certain types of sounds in "mood rooms" will be useful in elevating productivity in the workplace.

Chapter Twenty-One

Spirituality in Practice

> If you meditate on your ideal, you will acquire its nature.
> If you think of God day and night, you will acquire the nature
> of God.

Sri Ramakrishna

In addition to the ideas discussed previously, there are many practical ways to cultivate spiritual values in an organization's culture.

For example, people work best when they are calm and creative. These two ideas work hand in hand; one cannot be present without the other. The latest sports psychology employs the following fundamentals in a regimen to increase creativity and calm for maximizing productivity:

- Know your subject very well
- Exercise mental strength and flexibility
- Make recovery periods a habit

Source: Aon Consulting

When working, be intensely absorbed in the present moment, not concerning yourself with the future or the past. Apply creativity tactics in your work. Finally, recover often in small bits of time.

The winning companies of the future will facilitate this mode of working, and the results will show in the top line as well as the profits. For example, setting up "recovery rooms" as described in the chapter dealing with sense utilization will offer the relaxation periods needed by the body and mind for maximum productivity.

Being attentive to the present moment is the essential ingredient for producing results. Yesterday does not exist; tomorrow is merely a thought. The "now" moment is the only reality. Spending more time living in this moment, experiencing it in its fullness, will lead to magical results.

Creativity is the engine that churns the magical thoughts while being presenting aware. Use the tools that facilitate creative thought generation. Simply observing the object quietly for long periods of time provide the mind with the space to bubble up ideas. Free association and "free-writing" are also springboards in the creative process. Ironically, thinking of the least likely solutions is a best practice for producing winning ideas. The Post-It notes were created from this process, when an experimental glue failed the requirements dictated by the original purpose. But the inventor used the glue on paper to temporarily mark pages in the church choral books. Bingo. An idea that has revolutionized our lives both in the office and at home.

Creativity is the mother of invention. Out of the depths of silence arises form. Write down your creative thoughts—they are magical.

In the 1890s, William Wrigley decided on a whim to offer chewing gum as a premium for purchasing baking powder and soap. It was a big hit. Today, Wrigley's gum is sold in over 120 countries.

Night dreams are the magical, creative playground of the subconscious mind. Allow the power of the subconscious to work for you by journaling your dreams. They will provide you with unlimited insight.

Cultivate your memory

Learn to use and expand your memory. Using the creative techniques to develop memory will expand the mind. You will become more successful as a result.

Teach memory training in your organization. In a survey regarding a manager's ability to succeed, the single most important factor was memory.

How to be more effective in interaction

People are motivated by many things. Money, companionship, friendship, fear of being alone, and self-actualization are just some of the things that motivate people to act.

Psychologists generally agree that what causes one to act on something is a result of how that person perceives whether the action relates to pleasure or pain. That is, if a person believes that an action will increase pleasure or reduce pain, that individual will have a tendency to act accordingly.

This model will become less important as motivation becomes more universal. People are primarily motivated through three different media: visual, auditory and kinesthetic. You can determine an individual's primary mode of motivation by looking for clues. For example, a visually motivated person will tend to say things such as, "that proposal looks good to me." Or, "can you see what I'm saying?"

On the other hand, an auditory person may say, "that sounds good to me." Or, "Are you listening to me?" A kinesthetic person might say, "that feels right to me." Or, "that meal hit the right spot."

Rate of speech can also be a differentiating factor. In general, visually inclined people talk the fastest, and kinesthetically motivated people tend to speak the slowest. While this does not always hold true due to other factors, it is a good rule of thumb.

What is happening is that the person is expressing in the way he or she relates to the world. Body language is another expression that occurs on the physical level. For example, a visual person tends to look up or straight ahead, while the auditory person will glance side to side tilts his or her head toward the speaker, waiting for more verbal information. The kinesthetic person tends to look down, accessing from time to time how he or she feels about what is being expressed.

While this is a simplified primer on relational modes of behavior, you can use this information every day to interact more effectively with those around you. One way to use motivational modes is to work with the clues as you interact, without ever having to evaluate whether that individual is visual, auditory, or kinesthetic.

For example, you are discussing your weekend with Sally. She stares straight ahead toward you, occasionally asking about the details about your trip. You sense that Sally is visual, and you immediately pull out the pictures from last weekend. Bingo! Sally is even more interested in your trip.

You should learn the modes of influences for your key stakeholders, such as primary customers, managers and employees. By addressing their concerns and *how* you deliver those messages, you will become a more effective communicator. Spend more time preparing presentations and your part of discussions with the modes in which you will communicate. At certain times you will want to persuade a particular person, and therefore, gear your discussion toward that person accordingly.

Before key meetings, learn who those key stakeholders are and evaluate how each is influenced. The outcome will be more favorable, as you more effectively engage each participant in the meeting.

In a group setting, with people who represent each mode of influence, the way to approach presentations, meetings, or discussions is to proactively interweave the three modes continuously throughout your part of the interaction. By including all three modes and continuously changing between these modes of influence, you will engage the three types of people as you interact with them. The best speakers and presenters are able to do this with relative ease.

For example, if you are giving a sales presentation on the new model of pens to be introduced next year, include handouts and pen samples for the kinesthetic folks. They will be motivated by holding something. The visual people will be looking for beautiful, clear and concise charts. The auditory people will listen for words with zip and pizzazz. Omit the buzzwords, and you will lose your audience.

Develop communication skills

This idea is in line with how well information moves throughout the organization. The ability to communicate effectively is becoming increasingly important, as information is now probably the most important differentiating factor in an organization's success.

EPILOGUE

A hundred years from now, it won't matter how much money you made, what your net worth was, how many times you were promoted, or what your last title was. What will matter is how much love you shared on this planet. The love that you shared enables our transformation as spiritual beings.

Spiritual values are a function of love. Peace, compassion, a sense of unity *happen* when love is practiced in each moment. Love in all of her forms does not stop at the workplace. It must be a part of everything that we do.

My great friend and guru Billie Langnau once wrote, "Love is all there is." The absence of love is the beginning of violence, war, confusion . . . those things that are reminders to practice love.

Without spiritual values being the basis for everything that we do, we will perish. We will evolve to the point of continually thinking about our essential nature, our spiritual beingness. Automation is allowing that process to take place. More time is available to focus on our being, our awareness, our evolution.

Our spirituality is not a private matter. It must be the foundation for all we do. Each of us has a personal responsibility to live our lives spiritually wherever we are . . . including the workplace. When each of us practices our spiritual values, we transform the people and environment around us. Through the transformation of individuals, then groups of people, global transformation is happening. It is our destiny.

As each person makes steps to enact the vision that I have sketched in this book, they empower others to do the same. We belong to each other, and what affects one affects all. If you are reading this book, you have the power to transform your organization, and, through it, to transform the world.

You have perhaps already realized that spirituality is not something otherworldly, detached, and impractical. Rather, spirituality begins with the people and places that we encounter every day. As you put this book into practice, remember that each customer or client, each vendor or associate, each person, animal, plant and thing in your sphere of influence is another opportunity to bring love and concern into the world. When you care for others, you are caring for yourself, and when you care for yourself, you are caring for others.

Take this opportunity to make your life and work more positive, more values-oriented, and more centered and balanced. You will find that the journey is its own reward.

BIBLIOGRAPHY

Barrett, William. *The Illusion of Technique: A Search for Meaning in a Technological Civilization*. Norwell, MA: Anchor, 1979.

Ben & Jerry's. www.benjerry.com.

Body Shop, The. www.thebodyshop-usa.com.

Brazil. DVD. Directed by Terry Gilliam. 1985; Embassy International: Croydon, UK. Universal, 2007.

Brodsky, Norm. "The Best Laid Plans: A veteran CEO Explains why you have to know where you want to be before you let your company take you there." *Inc.* January 1997. 83.

Covey, Stephen. *The Seven Habits of Highly Effective People*. New York: Free Press, 2004.

Davidson, G.E. "The Quantity and Significance of Psychological Distress in Medical Patients: Some Preliminary Observations about the Decision to Seek Medical Aid." *Journal of Chronic Disease* 17 (Oct 1964): 959-970

Deming, W. Edward. *Out of the Crisis*. Cambridge, MA: MIT Press, 2000.

Edvinsson, Leif. Interviewed in *Fast Company*, February / March 1997. 58.

Maslow, Abraham. "A Theory of Human Motivation." *Psychological Review* 50, No. 4 (1943): 370-396.

Meyerson, Mort. Interviewed in *Fast Company*, February / March 1997. 99.

Miller, Henry. "On Writing." In *The Creative Process: Reflections on Invention in the Arts and Sciences*. Edited by Brewster Ghiselin. Berkeley: University of California Press, 1984.

Nesbitt, John and Patricia Aburdene. *Megatrends 2000*. New York: William Morrow, 2000.

Redfield, James. *The Celestine Prophecy*. New York: Warner, 1997.

Rifkin, Jeremy. *The Empathic Civilization: The Race to Global Consciousness in a World in Crisis*. New York: Tarcher: 2009.

Robbins, John. "Beginning with Love." In *Handbook for the Heart: Original Writings on Love*. Edited by Richard Carlson and Benjamin Shield. New York: Back Bay, 1998. 145-149.

Rosen, G., Kleinman, A., and Katon, W. "Somatization in Family Practice: A Biopsychosocial Approah." *Journal of Family Practice* 14 no. 3 (Mar 1982): 493-502

Schucman, Helen. *A Course in Miracles*. Mill Valley, CA: Foundation for Inner Peace, 2007.

Stevenson, Thomas G. "Transforming Business." PhenomeNews

Taylor, Jim. Interviewed in *Fast Company* January / February 1997. 85.

United Nations International Labor Organization. "Global Wage Report 2010/2011: Wage Policies in Times of Crisis." New York: 2010.

United States Bureau of Labor Statistics. News Release. "Employee Tenure in 2010." September 14, 2010.

United States Department of Agriculture. "United States Census of Agriculture 2008." February 4, 2009. www.agcensus.usda. gov.

Welwood, John. *Journey of the Heart: The Path of Conscious Love*. New York: Harper, 1990.

Williamson, Marianne. *Return to Love: Reflections on the Principles of A Course in Miracles*. New York: Harper, 1992. 190-191.

Zukav, Gary. *The Dancing Wu Li Masters: An Overview of the New Physics*. New York: Harper, 2001.